PARIS

|CONDENSED|

 rob flynn

LONELY PLANET PUBLICATIONS
Melbourne • Oakland • London • Paris

contents

Lonely Planet Condensed – Paris
1st edition – April 2000

Published by
Lonely Planet Publications Pty Ltd
A.C.N. 005 607 983
192 Burwood Rd, Hawthorn,
Victoria 3122, Australia

Lonely Planet Offices
Australia PO Box 617, Hawthorn, VIC 3122
USA 150 Linden St, Oakland, CA 94607
UK 10a Spring Place, London NW5 3BH
France 1 rue du Dahomey, 75011 Paris

Photographs
All of the images in this guide are available
for licensing from Lonely Planet Images.
email: lpi@lonelyplanet.com.au

Front cover photographs
Top: View of the Île de la Cité
    (Rob Flynn)
Bottom: Tour Eiffel detail
    (Richard I'Anson)

ISBN 1 86450 044 1

text & maps © Lonely Planet 2000
photos © photographers as indicated 2000

Printed by The Bookmaker Pty Ltd
Printed in China

how to use this book

KEY TO SYMBOLS

- ✉ address
- ☎ telephone number
- @ email/web site address
- Ⓜ nearest metro station
- 🚇 nearest train station
- 🚌 nearest bus route
- ✈ nearby airport
- ⓘ tourist information
- ☺ opening hours
- ⑤ cost, entry charge
- ♿ wheelchair access
- 👶 child-friendly
- ✗ on-site or nearby eatery
- Ⓥ vegetarian, or with a good vegetarian selection

COLOUR-CODING

Each chapter has a different colour code which is reflected on the maps for quick reference.

MAPS & GRID REFERENCES

The fold-out maps on the front and back covers are numbered from 1 to 5. All sights and venues in the text have map references which indicate where to find them, eg (3, H4) means Map 3, grid reference H4. When a map reference appears immediately after a name, the sight is labelled on the map; when it appears after an address (eg with most restaurants, hotels etc), only the street is marked.

PRICES

Multiple prices (eg 40/30/20FF) indicate adult/concession/student entry charges. Concession prices include youth and senior discounts; family discounts are rare. Entry charges are often lower on Sunday.

WARNING & REQUEST

Things change – prices go up, schedules change, good places go bad and bad places improve or go bankrupt. So, if you find things better or worse, recently opened or long since closed, please tell us and help make the next edition even more accurate and useful. Everyone who writes to us will find their name and possibly excerpts from their correspondence in one of our publications (let us know if you *don't* want your letter published or your name acknowledged). They will also receive the latest issue of *Planet Talk*, our quarterly printed newsletter, or *Comet*, our monthly email newsletter. Subscriptions to both newsletters are free. The very best contributions will be rewarded with a free guidebook.

Send all correspondence to the Lonely Planet office closest to you (see page 123).

Lonely Planet books provide independent advice. Lonely Planet does not accept advertising in guidebooks, nor payment in exchange for listing or endorsing any place or business. Lonely Planet writers do not accept discounts or payments in exchange for positive coverage of any sort.

facts about paris

Paris is the most seductive city on the planet, with beauty, art and romance in spades. But the idea of visiting the city can be intimidating. It's not just the acres of museums, imposing old buildings, and wall to wall art, culture and *haute couture* – it's the horror stories of cramped hotel rooms, rip-off prices and ill-mannered natives.

But Paris is no longer the living museum or Gallic theme park it may have seemed a generation ago. Paris has changed, and it's a welcoming, fun and increasingly cosmopolitan city to visit.

Do the sites, visit the museums – they're part of the experience. But then, jump on the metro or a bus and get off at a place you've never heard of, wander through a quarter where French mixes with Arabic or Vietnamese, poke your head into mysterious shops or just perch on a cafe terrace with a *café* or glass of wine and watch Paris pass by.

Parisians like to believe they have *savoir vivre* – the art of knowing how to live – and indeed you'll find that Paris is a feast for all the senses. It's a city to look at, with its

wide boulevards, impressive monuments, great works of art and magic lights. It's a city to taste: cheese, chocolate, wine, seafood, bread. It's a city to hear, whether you crave opera, jazz or rap. It's a city to smell: the perfume boutiques, fresh coffee and croissants in a morning cafe, roasting chestnuts in winter. It's a city to feel: the wind in your face as you rollerblade through Bastille or cycle along the Seine, or the giddy mixture of fear and pleasure as you peer out from atop the Tour Eiffel.

Above all, it's a city to discover. Read this book – it's designed to get you started – but leave it in your hotel from time to time, and wander outside to be seduced by your own Paris.

Paris panorama

HISTORY
The Gauls & the Romans
The Île de la Cité was settled during the 3rd century BC by a tribe of Celtic Gaul river-traders known as the Parisii. Centuries of conflict between the Gauls and Rome ended in 52 BC, when Julius Caesar's legions took control of the territory and established the Roman town of Lutetia on the island and the left (south) bank of the Seine.

In AD 508, the Frankish king Clovis I united Gaul as a kingdom and made Paris (as the town was now known) his capital. Despite a succession of raids by the Scandinavian Vikings during the 9th century, Paris soon prospered as the capital of the kingdom of Francia and a centre of politics, commerce, religion and culture.

My Kingdom for a Mass
When Paris' new Protestant king took the throne as Henri IV in 1589, the ultra-Catholic Parisians refused to allow him entry to the city, and a siege of the capital continued for almost 5 years. Only when Henri embraced Catholicism at Saint Denis did the capital submit to him. *'Paris vaut bien une messe'* (Paris is well worth a Mass), he is reputed to have said upon taking communion.

The Middle Ages
In the 12th century, construction began on the greatest creation of medieval Paris, the cathedral of Notre Dame (completed nearly 200 years later). The Marais (marsh) area north of the Seine was drained and the Right Bank developed as the town's mercantile centre. The food markets at Les Halles opened in 1110, and the Louvre was built as a riverside fortress in around 1200. Meanwhile, the area on the south bank of the Seine developed as a place of scholarship and learning, the Sorbonne opening its doors in 1253.

The Renaissance
Paris eagerly embraced the culture of the Italian Renaissance in the early 16th century, and many of the city's signature buildings and monuments sprang up during the period, including the Pont Neuf, the Église St-Eustache and the Hôtel (now Musée) Carnavalet. Henri IV (ruled 1589-1610) rebuilt Paris in grand style, including the magnificent Place Royal (now the Place des Vosges) and Place Dauphine.

Louis XIV & the Ancien Régime
Louis XIV, known as le Roi Soleil (the Sun King), ascended to the throne in 1643 at the tender age of 5 and held the Crown until 1715. During his reign, he nearly bankrupted the national treasury with prolonged bouts of battling and building. His most tangible legacy is the palace at Versailles, 23km south-west of Paris, but he also commissioned the fine Place Vendôme, Place des Victoires, Invalides and the Louvre's Cour Carrée.

A century later, the excesses of Louis XVI and his capricious queen, Marie-Antoinette, led to an uprising of Parisians on 14 July 1789 and the storming of the Bastille prison, the ultimate symbol of the despotism of the *ancien régime*. The French Revolution had begun.

Revolution & Napoleon

The moderate populist ideals of the Revolution's early stages quickly gave way to the Reign of Terror; over 17,000 people were introduced to madame la guillotine, including Louis XVI and his queen, and even many of the original 'patriots' such as Robespierre.

The unstable post-Revolution government was consolidated in 1799 under a young Corsican general, Napoleon Bonaparte. In 1804, Napoleon crowned himself Emperor of the French at Notre Dame, and proceeded to sweep most of Europe under his wing.

Colonne Vendôme, topped by Napoleon portrayed as Caesar

The Second Empire

Following Napoleon's exile to St Helena in 1815, France faltered under a string of mostly inept rulers until a coup d'état in 1851 ushered in the Second Empire and a new emperor, Napoleon III (nephew of Bonaparte). Napoleon III charged Baron Haussmann with the task of demolishing the old, cramped, dark and insanitary city in order to rebuild Paris as a great imperial capital. Over the next 18 years Haussmann transformed Paris into the city we recognise today, with its wide boulevards, fine public buildings and sculptured parks. The Garnier Opera House was the jewel in the new capital's crown.

Inevitably, Napoleon III's pugnacity led to a costly and eventually unsuccessful war with the Prussians in 1870. Napoleon III was captured and the masses took to the streets, demanding that a republic be declared. A battle for power ensued between supporters of the monarchist government and the republicans of the Paris Commune, who briefly took over Paris. Some 20,000 Communards were summarily executed during the insurrection.

La Marseillaise, *Arc de Triomphe*

The Belle Époque to the Present

Despite its bloody beginnings, the Third Republic ushered in the glittering *belle époque* (beautiful age), with its famed Art Nouveau architecture and a barrage of advances in the arts and sciences. The Tour Eiffel, impressionism and the Paris of nightclubs and artistic cafes are legacies of this time. By the 1920s and 30s, Paris had become a worldwide centre for the artistic and intellectual avant-garde.

I M Pei's glass pyramid, Musée du Louvre

Grande Arche de La Défense

The exuberance of the period was snuffed out by the Nazi occupation of Paris in 1940, which continued until 25 August 1944. Hitler, who strode beneath the Arc de Triomphe in June 1940, later ordered his retreating army to torch the city; happily, his general refused.

After the war, Paris regained its position as a creative hotbed and nurtured a revitalised liberalism that reached its crescendo in the student-led 'Spring Uprising' of 1968, when some 9 million people joined in a paralysing general strike sparked by opposition to the Vietnam War.

During the 1980s, President François Mitterrand initiated his visionary *grands travaux*, a series of ambitious building projects designed to transform the face of Paris. Responses to the most provocative designs, such as the Musée du Louvre's glass pyramid and the Grande Arche de La Défense, range from appalled to rapturous.

In July 1998, a million ecstatic Parisians choked the Champs Élysées following France's first-ever World Cup football victory. The against-the-odds win (3-0 over Brazil) by a mixed-race team was seen by many Parisians as a symbolic achievement of a newly self-confident, vigorous and pluralistic France.

ORIENTATION

Paris is a remarkably compact city (around 10km in diameter), built on the banks of the river Seine in the central north of France. The perimeter of the city is roughly defined by the blvd *périphérique*, the ring road which separates the city from the *banlieus* (suburbs), reached via Paris' 37 *portes* (gates).

Conventionally, the Seine divides the well-heeled Right Bank (*Rive Droite*), north of the river, from the more bohemian Left Bank (*Rive Gauche*) – though the reality, of course, is much more complex. On the Right Bank you'll find the Louvre, the Champs Élysées, the Marais and the most exclusive shopping districts; on the Left Bank you have the Quartier Latin, the Musée d'Orsay and blvds St-Michel and St-Germain.

Paris is divided into 20 numbered *arrondissements* (districts) that spiral clockwise from the city centre like a conch shell. While some Parisian neighbourhoods have names, most addresses simply refer to their arrondissement. The Tour Eiffel dominates the western end of the city, Montparnasse tower the south and Sacré Cœur the north, while Bastille is a useful landmark in the east.

ENVIRONMENT

For a densely populated, inland, urban centre, inhabited for more than 2 millennia, Paris is a surprisingly clean and healthy city. Thanks are due mainly to Baron Haussmann, who radically reshaped the city in the second half of the 19th century, widening streets, building parks, and modernising the sewer and storm-water systems.

Despite the city's excellent public transport system, Haussmann's wide boulevards are usually choked with traffic, and air pollution is undoubtedly the city's major environmental hazard. Second on the list is probably the noise generated by the same traffic – especially motorbikes and trucks (a pair of earplugs is a worthwhile investment for a sound night's sleep).

Fortunately, Parisians are rediscovering the *vélo* (bicycle), and a network of some 130km of city bicycle lanes has been created over the past few years. Car owners are encouraged to leave their vehicles at home on specially earmarked days.

Indoors, be prepared to inhale second-hand cigarette (and even cigar) smoke pretty much everywhere – including in restaurants and nonsmoking areas.

Steady efforts have been made to clean up the Seine – these days it's muddy rather than dirty.

Simon Bracken

Old-fashioned streetlamps at sunset

GOVERNMENT & POLITICS

Parisians love politics. Which is just as well, because there's no lack of politicians. Paris is home to the French president (Jacques Chirac), the prime minister (Lionel Jospin) and his government, the National Assembly, the Senate, the *maire* (mayor) of Paris (Jean Tiberi), the mayor's 18 *adjoints* (deputy mayors), the 163 members of the Conseil de Paris (Council of Paris), the mayors of each of the 20 arrondissements (plus their councils) and local European Parliament members.

Political debate is dominated by the right/left (*droite/gauche*), conservative/socialist divide, and there's a revolving door of personalities; Chirac, for instance, was mayor of Paris (the first actually elected since the Revolution) and prime minister before being elected president.

Parisian politics has always had a radical edge (ask Louis XVI), and it's not uncommon to hear nostalgic references to 1968, the year that violent student protests in Paris and general strikes brought down the De Gaulle government. Police in riot gear are still bussed in to 'control' the almost weekly peaceful *manifestations* (demonstrations) which rally at Bastille or République.

The Price of being Parisian

Average salaries range between 10,000 and 30,000FF per month. Employers pay an additional 40% of this amount into the French social security system, which covers unemployment benefits, health care and retirement pensions.

Monthly apartment rentals average around 100FF per sq m (an 80-sq-metre 2-bedroom apartment costs around 8000FF). The same apartment would probably cost more than a million francs to buy, depending on the location.

ECONOMY

Paris is predominantly a middle-class city, most of the workers having been pushed into the suburbs by rising rents. The city is the heart of France's commercial, industrial and financial sectors – about 20% of all economic activity in France takes place in the Paris region. A highly centralised bureaucracy means the capital also accounts for around 40% of the nation's white-collar jobs.

Sluggish economic growth – just under 3% in 1999 – has kept unemployment in France at around 11-12%, a figure that hasn't budged in years. There are estimated to be more than 50,000 *sans-abri* (homeless) on the streets of Paris; beggars are not uncommon.

Money, money, money

Penelope Richardson

SOCIETY & CULTURE

The population of Paris is about 2.2 million, while the Île de France (the greater metropolitan area of Paris) has about 10 million inhabitants – about 17% of France's total population of 58 million people. Paris today is a very cosmopolitan city, with many residents from other nations of the EU and a large English-speaking population.

In the second half of the 20th century France experienced waves of immigration, particularly from former French colonies in North Africa and French-speaking sub-Saharan Africa. During the late 1950s and early 60s, over 1 million French settlers returned to metropolitan France from Algeria, other parts of Africa and Indochina.

The French are generally more relaxed about relations between men and women – and about sex – than visitors might be accustomed to. Paris has thriving gay and lesbian communities, and same-sex couples are a common sight on its streets. Pigalle is the best known red light area; prostitution, though illegal, is tolerated and openly touted by streetwalkers in certain quarters of the city.

Etiquette

While the stereotype of the haughty, arrogant and unhelpful Parisian may have been accurate 20 years ago, it's certainly not true today. Parisians tend to be shy with strangers, but will readily help if approached in a friendly manner and with a word or two of imperfect French. As in other cities around the world, however, the more tourists a particular area or district attracts, the less patience the locals tend to have for them.

Parisian Etiquette

A few dos:

- Always say 'Bonjour' when you walk into a shop, and 'Merci, monsieur/madame/mademoiselle … au revoir' when you leave. 'Monsieur' means 'sir' and can be used with any male person who isn't a child. 'Madame' is used where 'Mrs' would apply in English, whereas 'mademoiselle' is used when talking to an unmarried woman. When in doubt, use 'madame'.

- If you want help or to interrupt someone, begin with 'Excusez-moi, monsieur/madame/mademoiselle'.

- It is customary for people who know each other to exchange *bises* (kisses) as a greeting, though rarely men with men unless they are close friends. The usual ritual is one glancing peck on each cheek. People who don't kiss each other will almost always shake hands.

A few don'ts:

- In a restaurant, do not summon the waiter by shouting 'garçon', which means 'boy'. Saying 's'il vous plaît' (please) is the way it's done nowadays.

- In general, lawns are meant to be looked at and praised for their greenness, not sat upon; watch out for *pelouse interdite* (Keep off the Grass!) signs.

ARTS

A century ago Paris held centre stage in the art world, attracting all manner of painters, writers and musicians. The period was merely one of many high points for a civilisation which for centuries has been synonymous with culture. Paris has held this reputation thanks in part to the city's peerless beauty, witnessed in its collection of exquisite historic buildings – the groundbreaking Gothic Notre Dame; ostentatiously baroque Palais du Luxembourg; seriously classical Panthéon and Arc de Triomphe; and breathtaking Art Nouveau detailing on everything from metro entrances to bistros.

The country's literary legacy is equally huge, from Molière, Racine, Voltaire and Rousseau to Hugo, Balzac, Zola, Proust, de Beauvoir and Camus.

The 19th century saw the rise of a number of musical luminaries such as Hector Berlioz, César Franck, George Bizet, Claude Debussy and Maurice

Pavement artist

Ravel. But it hasn't all been high culture: jazz hit Paris with a bang in the 1920s, producing violinist Stéphane Grappelli and legendary Gypsy guitarist Django Reinhardt, while popular singers who made an impact include Edith Piaf, Jacques Brel and Serge Gainsbourg.

France's place in film history was assured when the Lumière brothers invented 'moving pictures'; directors René Clair, Marcel Carné and Jean Renoir invented avant-garde cinema; Jean-Luc Godard, François Truffaut and Alain Resnais invented *nouvelle vague*; Jacques Tati invented Monsieur Hulot; and actors Anna Karina (*Alphaville*) and Jean-Paul Belmondo (*À Bout de Souffle*/Breathless) invented Parisian cool.

However, it's in the world of oils and watercolours that Paris has truly inspired. According to Voltaire it all began with Nicolas Poussin (1594-1665) and Claude Lorrain (1600-82), painters of eerily light-drenched classical scenes. The neoclassical and romantic movements soon put a stop to pastel hues, with David and Géricault painting enough house-sized historical pictures to fill the Louvre (almost). Things pastoral made a return with the Barbizon School of Corot and Millet, who gathered to paint in the open air (at that time a novel idea), and the idea really took off with the headline-grabbing impressionists, led by Claude Monet. Innovative artists inspired by the idea of capturing the fleeting effects of light included Sisley, Seurat, Pisarro, Renoir, Degas, Toulouse-Lautrec, Cézanne, Gauguin and Rousseau. Ensuing movements such as symbolism (Moreau), fauvism (Matisse and Derain), cubism (Braque) and dada (Duchamp) ensured that Paris' cafes, studios and attics were filled with artists, both French and foreign-born. In the 21st century, the city continues to be a spiritual home for artists, aesthetes and romantics alike.

highlights

Paris, like traditional French cuisine, has a surfeit of riches. Many visitors make the mistake of trying to taste everything in too short a time – the Louvre, the Tour Eiffel, the Centre Pompidou, Sacré Cœur, blvd St-Germain, the Arc de Triomphe – ending up with severe indigestion.

It's impossible to see everything that Paris has to offer on a short visit – so don't even try. Make sure you see the few sights you're really passionate about, and just get out there and explore.

Paris sees more tourists than just about any other city on earth, which means there'll be queues and crowds at all of the top attractions. If you plan to tackle the major sites, the best strategy is to

> ## Museums Pass
> If you plan to 'do' multiple museums and monuments over just a few days, or want to avoid long queues, invest in a **Carte Musée et Monuments** (80/160/240FF for 1/3/5 days), available from major metro stations, participating museums and tourist offices.

start early, pace yourself, and make sure you take a good book or fascinating companion to keep you occupied while queuing. Late in the day is also a good time to visit sites, but keep in mind that ticket sales usually stop 15-45mins before closing time.

Finally, don't miss seeing Paris by night. The river and monuments are transformed after dark, and even the traffic seems to add to the magic when viewed from afar.

Stopping Over?

One Day Start with a stroll around the Île de la Cité and Île St-Louis, not forgetting to pay your respects to Notre Dame; lunch on the terrace of La Samaritaine department store overlooking the Seine; head down to the Tour Eiffel for the view at dusk; cruise back up the river by boat before having dinner and a nightcap in the Marais.

> ## Paris Lowlights
> **Bastille** Paris' most famous monument that doesn't exist – the prison site is now a busy traffic roundabout.
>
> **Quartier Latin** Avoid the rip-off cafes and fast-food joints.
>
> **Sacré Cœur** Graceless and gloomy inside, but enchanting from a distance.
>
> **Mona Lisa** Small, glassed-in and surrounded by crowds.

Two Days Spend the morning at the Louvre or the Musée d'Orsay, according to taste; after a picnic lunch in the Square du Vert Galant, take an afternoon stroll around Montmartre and make a night of it at the restaurants and bars around Bastille or rue Oberkampf.

Three Days Shop! Head for the department stores near Opéra, browse the backstreets of the Marais or St-Germain, or raid the designer boutiques of rue St-Honoré and Place des Victoires. Visit a small museum – perhaps the Rodin or Cluny – and splurge at the most expensive traditional French restaurant you can afford.

ARC DE TRIOMPHE & CHAMPS ÉLYSÉES   (3, B2)

Napoleon's Arc de Triomphe towers 50m above Place Charles de Gaulle (or Place d'Étoile – 'Star Place'), the vast traffic roundabout from which 12 grand boulevards radiate. From the top of the arch (284 steps, and well worth the effort) you can look straight down the greatest of these boulevards, ave des Champs Élysées, to the Place de la Concorde.

INFORMATION

- ✉ Place Charles de Gaulle, 8e
- ☎ 01 55 37 73 77
- Ⓜ Charles de Gaulle-Étoile; George V; Franklin D Roosevelt; Champs Élysées Clemenceau
- 🚌 22, 30, 31, 52, 73, 92
- ⊘ Oct-Mar 10am-10.30pm; Apr-Sept 9.30am-11pm
- ⑤ 40/25FF
- ♿ limited

Richard J'Anson

Among the armies to march triumphantly through the arch and down the Champs Élysées were the Germans in 1871, the Allies in 1919, the Germans again in 1940 and the Allies in 1944. Since 1920, the body of an Unknown Soldier from the WWI battlefield of Verdun has lain beneath the arch.

The arch was commissioned by Napoleon in 1806 to commemorate his great battle victories, but was still under construction when he met his Waterloo in 1815; it was finally completed in 1836. The best known of the 4 high-relief panels (on the right as you face the arch from the Champs Élysées) is François Rude's *La Marseillaise*.

The 2km-long Champs Élysées was popular with the aristocracy of the mid-19th century as a stage on which to parade their wealth. Since WWII, it has been taken over by airline offices, cinemas, car showrooms and fast-food restaurants. The wealthy denizens of the exclusive **Triangle d'Or** area next door consider the Champs Élysées to be completely degraded and popularised (by which they mean the same thing). In the last few years beautification works have returned some of the former sparkle and prestige to the avenue.

Martin Moos

Arc de Triomphe

CENTRE POMPIDOU (5, B7)

The Centre Georges Pompidou (also known as the Centre Beaubourg) has amazed and delighted visitors since it was built in the mid-1970s – not just for its outstanding collection of modern art, but for its radical (at the time) architectural statement.

In order to keep the exhibition halls as spacious and uncluttered as possible, the architects – the Italian Renzo Piano and Briton Richard Rogers – put the building's 'insides' on the outside. The purpose of each of the ducts, pipes and vents that enclose the centre's glass walls can be divined from the paint job: escalators and lifts in red, electrical circuitry in yellow, the plumbing green and the air-conditioning system blue. The building reopened on the first day of the new millennium after a 2-year refit, with new exhibition spaces – and a new coat of paint.

The Pompidou attracts around 25,000 visitors a day, thanks in part to its vigorous schedule of outstanding temporary exhibitions. Two floors are dedicated to exhibiting some of the 40,000-plus works of the **Musée National d'Art Moderne (MNAM)**, France's national collection of 20th-century art – including the fauves, the surrealists, cubists, pop art and contemporary works.

The **Atelier Brancusi**, the studio of the Romanian-born sculptor Constantin Brancusi (1876-1957), contains almost 140 examples of his work as well as drawings, paintings and glass photographic plates.

The open spaces around the centre – especially **Place Igor Stravinsky** – are filled with modern sculpture, street performers and gawkers, and are as much fun as the centre itself.

INFORMATION

✉ rue St-Martin, 4e
☎ 01 44 78 12 33
Ⓜ Rambuteau
🚌 21, 29, 38, 47, 58, 69, 70, 72, 74, 75, 76, 81, 85, 96
🕐 11am-10pm (closed Tues)
$ 30/20FF-50/40FF, depending on exhibitions chosen; under 18 free to MNAM; under 13 free to exhibitions
@ www.centrepompidou.fr
♿ OK, access through Atelier Brancusi
✗ restaurant & cafe

Olivier Cirendini

Rod Hyett

Centre Pompidou's external pipes

DON'T MISS
• wacky Fontaine Stravinsky • view from the rooftop terrace
• street theatre and buskers

CIMETIÈRE DU PÈRE LACHAISE   (2, E13)

Founded in 1804, Père Lachaise Cemetery is the most visited necropolis in the world. Its 70,000 ornate (and at times ostentatious) tombs of the rich and/or famous form a verdant, open-air sculpture garden.

Simon Bracken

Among the 1 million people buried here are the composer Chopin; the writers Molière, Apollinaire, Oscar Wilde, Balzac, Marcel Proust, Gertrude Stein (and Alice B Toklas) and Colette; artists David, Delacroix, Pisarro, Seurat and Modigliani; actors Sarah Bernhardt, Simone Signoret and Yves Montand; singer Edith Piaf; dancer Isadora Duncan; and even those immortal 12th-century lovers Abélard and Héloïse, the cemetery's oldest residents.

Most young visitors make a beeline for the Division 6 grave of 1960s rock star **Jim Morrison**, lead singer of the Doors, who died (or did he?) in an apartment on rue Beautreillis in the Marais in 1971.

On 27 May 1871, the last of the Communard insurgents, cornered by government forces, fought a hopeless, all-night battle among the tombstones. In the morning, the 147 survivors were lined up against the **Mur des Fédérés** (Federalists' Wall) and shot. They were buried in a mass grave where they fell.

The cemetery has 4 entrances, 2 of them on blvd de Ménilmontant. Maps indicating the location of noteworthy graves are posted around the cemetery and can be obtained free from the Conservation office. Newsstands and kiosks in the area sell the more detailed *Plan Illustré du Père Lachaise* (Illustrated Map of Père Lachaise), which is worth the small asking price if you're interested in exploring for an hour or two.

People are still dying to get into Père Lachaise: the cemetery caters for around 1000 burials and 4000 cremations a year.

Necrophilia

Oscar Wilde's tomb features a carved angel whose genitals were considered so obscene they were hacked off and used as a paperweight by the cemetery's director. Meanwhile, those on the effigy of Victor Noir are noticeably intact and are rubbed by wishful-thinking passers-by.

Martin Moos

Oscar Wilde's strangely exotic tomb

LA DÉFENSE   (2, B1)

La Défense is where Paris puts all those buildings other cities put downtown. Here you'll find all the concrete, glass and steel your big-city heart desires – but with a very French twist. Set on the banks of the Seine, just to the west of the 17e *arrondissement*, it puts a radically different perspective on 21st-century Paris.

One of the world's most ambitious urban construction projects, La Défense (named after the monument on the site commemorating the 1871 defence of Paris from the Prussians) was begun in the late 1950s. Some 60 gleaming skyscrapers housing corporate head offices and high-tech government institutions populate the 80-hectare site.

The remarkable **Grande Arche**, surely one of the weirdest buildings on earth, is the biggest drawcard. Designed by Danish architect Otto von Spreckelsen, it's a hollow cube of white marble and glass measuring 112m on each side – large enough to contain Notre Dame. One of Mitterrand's *grands projets*, it was opened on 14 July 1989, and forms the current western terminus of the 8km-long **Grand Axe** (Great Axis), which stretches from the Louvre's glass pyramid through the Jardin des Tuileries and along ave des Champs Élysées to the Arc de Triomphe, Porte Maillot and finally the fountains, squares and plazas of La Défense's **Esplanade du Général de Gaulle**. The structure, symbolising a window open to the world, is slightly out of alignment with the Grand Axe.

INFORMATION

☎ 01 49 07 27 27
  (La Grande Arche)
Ⓜ La Defénse Grande
  Arche
🚌 73
🕐 Grande Arche 10am-
  7pm
⑤ Grande Arche
  43/33FF
ⓘ Info Défense
  ☎ 01 47 74 84 24,
  15 Place de la
  Défense, 10am-6pm;
  guides available
🖥 www.grandearche.
  com

Skyscraper, or gratte-ciel ('scratch-sky'), La Défense

In a brave attempt to humanise the district's overwhelming corporate feel, the Esplanade and **Parvis** pedestrian precincts are now a **garden of contemporary art** featuring 70 monumental sculptures and murals, including colourful and imaginative works by Calder, Miró and Agam.

DON'T MISS
- CNIT, and Fiat, Manhattan and Elf office buildings
- Dôme IMAX cinema • Musée de l'Automobile

HÔTEL DES INVALIDES (3, F5)

The Hôtel des Invalides was built by Louis XIV in the 1670s as a kind of self-contained residential village for up to 4000 *invalides* (disabled veterans); a hundred or so vets are still housed here. The Cour d'Honneur courtyard serves as a venue for military parades, overlooked by a statue of Napoleon, affectionately known as the **Little Corporal**.

INFORMATION

- ✉ Esplanade des Invalides, 7e
- ☎ 01 44 42 37 72
- Ⓜ La Tour Maubourg
- ⒭ RER Invalides
- 🚌 82, 92
- ⏱ Napoleon's tomb 15 June-15 Sept 10am-6.45pm
- Ⓢ 37/27FF tomb and museum
- ⒠ www.invalides.org
- ✗ cafeteria

John Hay

In the centre of the compound is the glorious **Église du Dôme** (Dome Church), named for its gilded dome which is a glittering landmark. The church, considered one of the finest religious buildings built under Louis XIV, was constructed between 1677 and 1735; the dome itself took 27 years to build. It was intended for the king's own use and as a royal mausoleum, but instead the church became a mausoleum for military leaders.

In 1861 the Dome Church became home to **Napoleon's tomb**, Napoleon having died on St Helena 40 years earlier. It's an impressive final resting place: Napoleon's body is encased in no fewer than 5 coffins and a sarcophagus of red porphyry, displayed in an open crypt right under the dome. Other famous personages buried in the church include Napoleon's brother Joseph, military engineer Vauban and WWI hero Marshal Foch.

To Arms, Citizens

Unfortunately for Louis XIV's descendants, the Hôtel des Invalides played a key role in the events of 14 July 1789: the Paris mob forced their way into the building and, after fierce fighting, seized 28,000 rifles before heading on to the Bastille prison on the other side of the city. The rest, as they say ...

The buildings on either side of the **Cour d'Honneur** house the **Musée de l'Armée**, a huge museum of military history from the Stone Age to the end of WWII.

Diana Mayfield   Richard I'Anson

(L) Napoleon's Tomb (R) The Dome Church peers over the surrounding rooftops

JARDIN DU LUXEMBOURG   (5, C2)

When the weather is sunny – or even just not so overcast – Parisians of all ages flock to the formal Franco-Italian-style terraces and chestnut groves of the 25-hectare Jardin du Luxembourg (Luxembourg Gardens) to read, write, relax and sunbathe.

Napoleon dedicated the gardens to the children of Paris, and the gardens still offer all the delights of a Parisian childhood of a century ago. Join *les gosses* (the kids) and rent a **model sailing boat** at the Grand Bassin (the octagonal pond), or cheer the *guignol* (marionettes) at the pint-sized **Théâtre du Luxembourg** – even if you don't understand French.

Next door, there's the modern **playground**, vintage **swings** and an old-time **carousel** (merry-go-round). And 100m north of the theatre, kids of up to 35kg can ride Shetland ponies.

In the north-west corner of the gardens, **chess and card games** – often a dozen at a time – are held every afternoon of the year, rain or shine; BYOB (bring your own board). On the north side of the theatre, there are **basketball** and **volleyball** courts, or try inviting yourself to a game of *boules* (traditional bowling). There's a popular **jogging track** around the perimeter.

Less active visitors can simply enjoy the wonderful floral displays (best in spring) or bone-up on their bee-keeping skills at the **apiary**. The ancient **verger** contains around 200 varieties of pear and apple trees.

The **Palais du Luxembourg** is at the park's northern edge, with the Italianate Fontaine des Médicis (1642) nearby. The **Musée du Luxembourg** hosts temporary art exhibits, often from different regions of France.

INFORMATION

- ✉ blvd St-Michel, rue de Vaugirard, rue Guynemer, 6e
- ☎ 01 42 34 20 00
- Ⓜ Odéon
- Ⓡ RER Luxembourg
- ◷ Apr-Oct 7.30am-9.30pm; Nov-Mar 8am-5pm; marionettes Wed & Sat-Sun 3-4pm
- Ⓢ Gardens free; playgrounds 14FF; swings or carousel 7FF; pony rides 13FF; boats 17FF/hr; marionettes 22FF
- ⓘ Théâtre du Luxembourg ☎ 01 43 26 46 47; Palais du Luxembourg ☎ 01 42 34 20 60
- ♿ OK
- ✕ cafe

Pigeon Pie

As a struggling (and usually famished) young writer, Ernest Hemingway would visit the gardens for dinner – not to build up an appetite by looking at the flowers, but to catch pigeons and take them home to eat.

MARAIS (5, C8)

The Marais, the area of the Right Bank directly north of Île St-Louis, is a hip quarter of bars, cafes, art galleries, bookshops and boutiques; it's also the centre of Paris' gay life. On Friday and Saturday nights, the Marais is crowded with people out dining, bar-hopping and generally carousing.

INFORMATION

✉ 3e & 4e
Ⓜ Hôtel de Ville;
  St Paul; Bastille

Just 20 years ago, the Marais was one of the most neglected neighbourhoods of Paris – in spite of the fact that it had retained almost all of its pre-Revolutionary architecture. In the early 1600s, Henri IV built the Place Royal (now the Place des Vosges), creating Paris' most fashionable residential district. Wealthy aristocrats built their luxurious but subtle **hôtels particuliers** (private mansions) nearby; many of these now house museums and government institutions – the **Musée Picasso**, the **Musée Carnavalet** and the **Archives Nationales** are fine examples.

The elegant **Place des Vosges** is a quadrangle of 36 symmetrical houses with ground-floor arcades, steep slate roofs and large dormer windows. The park in the centre was once used for jousting and fighting duels, but today the park and arcades are used for more refined pursuits. The **Maison de Victor Hugo** at 6 Place des Vosges is where Victor Hugo lived from 1832 to 1848, and it is now a museum.

The Marais has a long-established **Jewish quarter** around the rue des Rosiers and rue des Écouffes. The **synagogue** in rue Pavée was designed by Hector Guimard.

Across rue du Rivoli, the streets of **Village St-Paul** have a similar medieval feel to the Marais, and are lined with interesting bars, restaurants, galleries and antique shops.

See page 49 for a walk around the Marais.

Place des Vosges' peerless symmetry

• Hôtel de Sully • a nightcap at *Le Petit Fer à Cheval*
• boutiques along rue Vieille du Temple and rue des Francs Bourgeois

MONTMARTRE & SACRÉ CŒUR (4, C6)

As you elbow your way through the gaggle of bus-delivered tourists paying outrageous prices for corny, mass-produced paintings in the **Place du Tertre**, it's difficult to imagine Van Gogh, Renoir, Picasso and Dalí setting up their easels here to change the face of modern art.

Despite the throngs, the **Butte de Montmartre** (Montmartre Hill, the highest point in Paris) retains much of its bohemian village feel. In its twisting, narrow streets you'll find Paris' 2 surviving **windmills** (4, B4), and sole **vineyard** (4, B5; on rue des Saules). Lose yourself in the area's **cobblestone streets**, far from the Paris of traffic and crowds.

For a more satisfying art fix, visit the **Espace Montmartre Salvador Dalí** (4, C5) or the **Musée d'Art Naïf Max Fourny** (4, D7). The **Bateau Lavoir** (4, C5), at 13 Place Emile Goudeau, was where Picasso, Braque, Gris, Modigliani and Apollinaire shared digs, and the **Lapin Agile** (4, B5; 26 rue des Saules) was where they caroused. **Van Gogh's House** was at No 54 rue Lepic, while the **Cimetière de Montmartre** residents include Emile Zola, Edgar Degas, François Truffaut and Vaslav Nijinsky.

The immense wedding-cake church perched on the summit of the butte is the modern **Basilique du Sacré Cœur** (Basilica of the Sacred Heart), consecrated in 1919. While it's worth a cursory glance inside, the steps are where the action takes place – lovers, buskers, locals and foreigners come here to take in the vistas and photograph each other. Ancient **St-Pierre de Montmartre**, adjacent to the basilica, is a more tranquil spot.

Rob Flynn

INFORMATION

- Ⓜ Abbesses; Blanche; Pigalle
- 🚌 30, 54, 67, 80, 95

Sacré Cœur's photogenic domes

Headless on Montmartre

Saint Denis, patron saint of France, introduced Christianity to Paris in the 2nd century. He was beheaded by the Romans on the hill now named Montmartre (Martyr Hill). You'll often see statues of him holding his head under his arm (for example on Notre Dame's portal).

Just a few blocks from the quiet residential streets of Montmartre is the lively, late-night/red-light neighbourhood of **Pigalle** (4, E3), where the can-can is *still* in vogue at the **Moulin Rouge** (4, D3).

For a walk around Montmartre, see page 51.

MUSÉE D'ORSAY (3, E8)

While the Musée d'Orsay plays second fiddle to the irresistible Louvre, most visitors find it a much more accessible and rewarding museum – mostly for its superb collection of French impressionist and post-impressionist works.

INFORMATION

- ✉ 1 rue de la Légion d'Honneur, 7e
- ☎ 01 40 49 48 14, 01 45 49 11 11 (recording)
- Ⓜ Solférino
- 🚆 RER Musée d'Orsay
- 🚌 24, 63, 68, 69, 73, 83, 84, 94
- ⏰ Tues-Sun 10am-6pm (Thurs to 9.45pm; Sun & June-Sept from 9am)
- 💲 40/30FF
- ⓘ English-language tours Tues-Sat 11am, Thurs 7pm 40FF; recorded tours (1½ hours) 30FF
- 🌐 www.musee-orsay.fr
- ♿ OK
- ✕ Café des Hauteurs

Musée d'Orsay

Bethune Carmichael

The museum displays France's national collection of paintings, sculptures, *objets d'art* and other works produced between 1848 (the proclamation of France's Second Republic) and 1914 (the beginning of the Great War). Its collection fits neatly between that of the Louvre and that of the Musée National d'Art Moderne at the Centre Pompidou.

The key works are on the ground floor (1848-1870) and the upper level (1870-1914). But don't bypass the Rodin sculptures (*Balzac* and *Gates of Hell*) and Art Nouveau collection on the middle level.

The ground floor has an eclectic sculpture gallery; Rude's *Spirit of the Fatherland* is a fragment of his famous *Marseillaise* relief for the Arc de Triomphe, while Carpeaux's exuberant *The Dance* scandalised Paris in 1868. Smaller galleries to each side feature key works from the classical and realist movements, including Ingre's *La Source* and Millet's *The Gleaners*, and some early 'impressionist' works such as Manet's provocative *Olympia* and *Déjeuner sur l'herbe*.

The upper level contains the museum's jewels: dozens of vibrant impressionist and neoimpressionist works, including Renoir's *Dancing at the Moulin de la Galette*, Degas' *Dance Class*, Monet's *Cathedral of Rouen* series and views of Giverny, Van Gogh's self-portraits and *Room at Arles*, and Cézanne's *Card Players*, plus major works by Pisarro, Manet, Whistler (yes, his *Mother*), Gauguin, Sisley and others.

For a breath of fresh air, the **terrace** has a great aspect over the Seine and a close-up view of the former station's enormous **clock**.

MUSÉE DU LOUVRE (3, E9)

The Louvre may be the world's greatest art museum – but it's probably also the one most avoided by visitors to Paris. Daunted by its sheer size (nearly 750m along the Seine) and overwhelming richness, many people find an afternoon at a smaller gallery far more inviting. But if you have even the merest interest in the fruits of human civilisation from antiquity to the 19th century, then visit you must.

To make your visit more enjoyable, pick up one of the useful map-guides and check out the works you *really* want to see, concentrating on only a couple of sections of the museum – and pretend that the rest is somewhere across town.

The most famous works from antiquity include the *Seated Scribe*, the *Jewels of Rameses II* and the armless duo – the *Winged Victory of Samothrace* and the *Venus de Milo*. From the Renaissance, don't miss Michelangelo's *Slaves*, Leonardo da Vinci's *Mona Lisa* and works by Raphael, Botticelli and Titian. French masterpieces of the 19th century include Ingres' *La Grande Odalisque*, Géricault's *The Raft of the Medusa* and the work of David and Delacroix.

The former fortress began its career as a public museum in 1793 with 2500 paintings; now some 30,000 are on display. The 7 billion FF Grand Louvre project has breathed new life into the museum with many new and renovated galleries now open to the public.

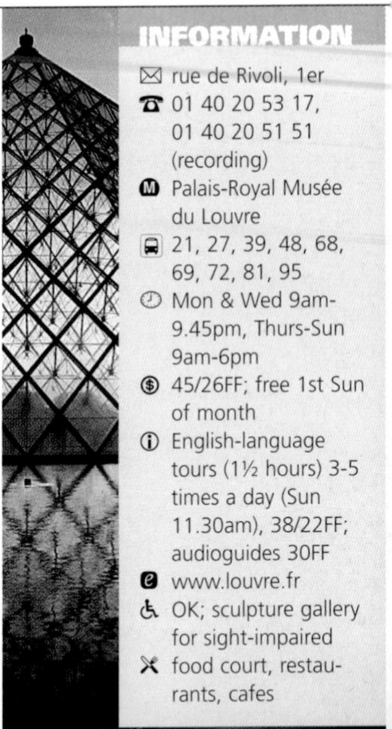

INFORMATION

- ✉ rue de Rivoli, 1er
- ☎ 01 40 20 53 17, 01 40 20 51 51 (recording)
- Ⓜ Palais-Royal Musée du Louvre
- 🚌 21, 27, 39, 48, 68, 69, 72, 81, 95
- ⊘ Mon & Wed 9am-9.45pm, Thurs-Sun 9am-6pm
- Ⓢ 45/26FF; free 1st Sun of month
- ⓘ English-language tours (1½ hours) 3-5 times a day (Sun 11.30am), 38/22FF; audioguides 30FF
- ℮ www.louvre.fr
- ♿ OK; sculpture gallery for sight-impaired
- ✗ food court, restaurants, cafes

Leda and the Swan, *Musée du Louvre*

Richard I'Anson

Greg Elms

DON'T MISS • I M Pei's glass pyramid • Cour Carrée by night • Richelieu Wing sculpture gardens • Sackler Wing of Oriental Antiquities

MUSÉE PICASSO (5, D8)

Not only was Pablo Picasso arguably the outstanding genius of 20th-century art, his capacity to work was superhuman: he painted, drew and made things from his early youth until his death, aged nearly 90. His legacy is vast, and much of it can be found in the wonderful Musée Picasso – one of Paris' best loved art museums.

INFORMATION

✉ 5 rue de Thorigny, 3e
☎ 01 42 71 25 21
Ⓜ St-Paul; Chemin Vert
🕐 Wed-Mon 9.30am-
   6pm (Thurs to 8pm)
⑤ 30/20FF
♿ OK
✕ cafe in summer

Martin Moos

Simon Bracken

Pondering Picasso

Although Picasso (1881-1973) was Spanish, he spent his artistically formative (and *transform*ative) early years and much of his later life in Paris. When he died, his family donated a quarter of his entire collection of drawings, engravings, paintings, ceramic works and sculptures to the French government in lieu of inheritance taxes.

In 1985 the government inaugurated the Musée Picasso to display the collection. Although none of his most celebrated works are here, the museum is still the world's most comprehensive overview of Picasso's oeuvre, and demonstrates, above all, his playfulness and humour.

The 200 paintings of the collection are arranged chronologically, moving through Picasso's early Blue and Rose periods, to the development and flowering of cubism and pieces from his later years. Some 3000 drawings and engravings give an insight into the artistic methods and prodigious output of the man, while more than 100 ceramic works and sculptures (many in the garden) demonstrate his mastery of a wide variety of media.

Tucked away in the Marais, the museum is handsomely curated in the Hôtel Salé, a carefully restored mid-17th-century mansion built by salt-tax collector Aubert de Fontenay. Many of the fine fixtures and pieces of furniture were designed by Diego Giacometti.

The museum also includes the Picasso Donation – part of Picasso's personal collection, featuring works by Cézanne, Braque, Matisse and Degas.

DON'T MISS
• Blue Period *Self-Portrait* • *Demoiselles d'Avignon* drawings
• *Still Life with Cane Chair* • *Young Girl Skipping Rope*
• *Baboon* sculpture with Citroën nose

MUSÉE RODIN (3, F6)

Decidedly one of the most tranquil spots in the city, the Musée Rodin is also many visitors' favourite Paris museum. When he died, the renowned sculptor Auguste Rodin (1840-1907) left his magnificent 18th-century residence and a huge body of work to the state in lieu of rent. Rooms on 2 floors of the house display extraordinarily vital bronze and marble sculptures, including casts of some of Rodin's most celebrated works: *The Hand of God*, *St John the Baptist*, *Balzac*, *Cathedral* and *The Kiss*.

Also on display are works by Rodin's model and lover, Camille Claudel (1864-1943), whose more gentle talent was overwhelmed by Rodin's prodigious genius (and his matching temperament). She spent the last 30 years of her life in madness in an asylum on Île St-Louis, unable to work. *L'Age Mûr* (Maturity) is a reflection of her torturous relationship with Rodin; the old woman is his wife.

The museum is housed in the Hôtel Biron, a private residence built for a wealthy wig-maker in 1728, and bearing the name of a general who lived here before being guillotined in 1793.

The delightful English-style **rose garden** (the third-largest private garden in Paris) is filled with shade trees and sculptures, including the original version of the work everyone comes to see, *The Thinker*.

Other celebrated works in the garden are *The Burghers of Calais* and the unfinished *Gates of Hell*, which kept Rodin occupied for the last 37 years of his life.

INFORMATION

- ✉ 77 rue de Varenne, 7e
- ☎ 01 44 18 61 10
- Ⓜ Varenne
- 🚌 28, 49, 69, 82, 92
- 🕐 9.30am-5.45pm (winter to 4.45pm)
- 💲 28/18FF; gardens only 5FF
- ♿ limited
- ✕ Cafétéria du Musée Rodin

Martin Moos

Martin Moos

Musée Rodin's spacious hôtel and gardens

Thoughtless Step

Rodin's most famous work, *Le Penseur* (The Thinker), was originally intended to grace the steps of the Panthéon – the mausoleum of France's greatest thinkers. But it was rejected by the City of Paris after a full-scale model was pilloried by the public and the press, and attacked by a madman with a hatchet.

NOTRE DAME   (5, C5)

If Paris has a heart, then this is it. Notre Dame de Paris (Our Lady of Paris) is not only a masterpiece of French Gothic architecture, but has also been Catholic Paris' ceremonial focus for 7 centuries.

Greg Elms

Bethune Carmichael

Notre Dame's portal statues

INFORMATION

- ✉ Place du Parvis, 4e
- ☎ 01 42 34 56 10
- Ⓜ Cité
- 🚍 21, 24, 27, 38, 47, 85, 96
- ⏰ cathedral 8am-7pm (closed Sat 12.30-2pm); towers 9.30am-7.30pm (Oct-Mar 10am-5pm); crypt 10am-6pm (Oct-Mar to 5pm); Sun Mass 10 & 11.30am, 12.30pm
- 💲 cathedral free; towers and crypt 35/23FF each or 50FF combined
- ⓘ free English-language tours Wed-Thurs noon, Sat 2.30pm (daily Aug)
- ♿ OK for cathedral

Built between 1163 and 1345 on a site occupied first by a Roman temple then by 2 earlier Christian churches, the cathedral was badly damaged following the Revolution; extensive renovations were made in the 19th century, partly due to the goading of Victor Hugo in his novel *The Hunchback of Notre Dame*.

The building is remarkable for its sublime balance, although if you look closely you'll notice minor asymmetrical elements introduced to avoid monotony. The cathedral's immense interior, a marvel of medieval engineering, can accommodate over 6000 worshippers. Exceptional features include the 7800-pipe **organ** and the spectacular **rose windows**, the most renowned of which are the window over the west façade (a full 10m across) and that on the north side of the transept, which has remained virtually unchanged since the 13th century.

Climbing the 387 steps of the **north tower** (entrance on rue du Cloître Notre Dame) brings you to the top of the **west façade**, where you'll find yourself face to face with many of the cathedral's most frightening gargoyles, which enjoy a spectacular view of Paris.

The best view of the **flying buttresses** – a Gothic technical innovation used to support the sheer walls and roof of the chancel – is from **Square Jean XXIII**, the lovely little park behind the cathedral.

DON'T MISS
- Crypte Archéologique
- free organ recitals (Sunday 5.45pm)

PARC DE LA VILLETTE (2, A13)

This futuristic park in the city's forgotten far-north-eastern corner is a playground for kids and adults alike. The park opened in 1993, and its lawns are enlivened by walkways, imaginative public furniture, a series of themed gardens and whimsical bright-red building-sculptures, known as *folies*. Attractions for the kids include a **merry-go-round**, a **playground** and 2 large play areas.

The centrepiece of the park, however, is the enormous **Cité des Sciences et de l'Industrie**, an interactive science museum, complete with planetarium, aquarium, cinema and multimedia library.

The adjacent **Géode** is a spectacular 36m-diameter sphere, whose mirror-like surface (made up of thousands of highly polished, stainless-steel triangles) has made it one of the architectural calling cards of modern Paris. Inside is an Omnimax cinema, where high-resolution films projected onto a semispherical, 180° screen give viewers a real sense of being part of the action (45min films every hour).

The **Cinaxe**, nearby, is a 60-seat hydraulic cinema that moves in synchronisation with the action on the screen (space flight, Formula 1 racing etc). Five-minute films are shown every 15mins.

The **Cité de la Musique**, towards the south of the park, houses a **music museum** with over 4500 instruments from the 16th century until today, a **concert hall** and the Paris National Conservatory of Dance and Music.

INFORMATION

- ⊠ 30 ave Corentin-Cariou, 19e
- ☎ 01 40 05 25 00 (Cité des Sciences et de l'Industrie and Géode), 01 44 84 44 84 (Cité de la Musique)
- Ⓜ Porte de la Villette; Porte de Pantin
- 🚌 75, 150, 152, 250A
- ◷ Cité des Sciences et de l'Industrie Tues-Sun 10am-6pm (Sun to 7pm); Géode 10am-9pm; Cinaxe 11am-6pm
- Ⓢ Cité Pass 50/35FF; Cité des Enfants 25FF adult +2 children; Cinaxe 25FF
- ⓘ Information Folie ☎ 01 40 03 75 03
- ⓔ www.la-villette.fr; www.cite-sciences.fr; www.cite-musique.fr
- ♿ OK
- ✗ cafes and fast-food folie

Martin Moos

Olivier Cirendini

Parc de la Villette's futuristic architecture

DON'T MISS
• open-air cinema • Jardin des Frayeurs Enfantines (Garden of Childhood Frights) • Cité des Enfants • Maison de la Villette – history of the site • *Bicyclette Ensevelie* (Buried Bicycle) sculpture

QUARTIER LATIN (5, D3)

The Latin Quarter – an area roughly encompassed by blvd St-Germain, rue Monge, rue Claude Bernard and blvd St-Michel – was the centre of the Roman town of Lutetia some 1800 years ago. However, the epithet 'latin' refers not to the Romans but to the language used between students and professors when this area was an important centre of learning during the Middle Ages – typified by the **Sorbonne**, the seat of the University of Paris. The only surviving remains of Roman Lutetia are the **Gallo-Roman baths** near the **Hôtel de Cluny** (5, C4), dating from around AD 200, and the **Arènes de Lutèce** (3, J12) theatre, unearthed in 1869.

INFORMATION

Ⓜ St-Michel; Cluny La Sorbonne; Cardinal Lemoine; Luxembourg

Today students and tourists are about an even mix on the quarter's main drags, **blvd St-Michel** (popularly known as the 'Boul Mich') and bustling **blvd St-Germain**, with their overpriced cafes, bookshops and American clothing stores.

The imposing **Panthéon** (5, D3) stands on the highest point on the Left Bank, and has superb views over central and eastern Paris. Adjacent is the beautiful 16th-century **Église St-Étienne du Mont**, home to the tomb of Sainte Geneviève, the patron saint of Paris.

Rue Mouffetard, winding down the hill from delightful **Place de la Contrescarpe** (5, E3), is one of the oldest, narrowest and liveliest streets in Paris. If you don't mind bumper-to-bumper tourists, wander along medieval **rue de la Harpe** and **rue de la Huchette**. Catch your breath in **Square René Viviani** (3, G11), and don't miss **Église St-Séverin** (5, C4) and little **St-Julien-le-Pauvre**, which claims to be Paris' oldest church (4th century) and has a fabulous view of Notre Dame.

See page 50 for a walk around the Left Bank.

The landmark Panthéon dominates the Left Bank

SAINTE CHAPELLE   (5, B5)

The most exquisite of Paris' Gothic monuments is tucked away within the walls of the **Palais de Justice** (Law Courts).

In stark contrast to the buttressed bulk of nearby Notre Dame, Sainte Chapelle is a masterpiece of delicacy and finesse. The 'walls' of the **upper chapel** (built for worship by the king and his court) are sheer curtains of richly coloured and finely detailed **stained glass**, which bathe the chapel in an extraordinary light. Designed in medieval times to inspire religious awe, the effect is still mesmerising.

INFORMATION

✉ Palais de Justice, blvd du Palais, 1er
☎ 01 53 73 78 50
Ⓜ Cité
🚌 21, 27, 38, 85, 96
🕐 Apr-Sept 9.30am-6.30pm; Oct-Mar 10am-5pm
💲 35/23FF
♿ limited

The windows depict biblical scenes, from Genesis (on the left as you enter the chapel from the spiral staircase) to the Apocalypse (the **rose window** behind you). The windows directly behind the altar depict Christ's Passion. Some 720 of the 1134 scenes depicted in the windows are the original stained glass – the oldest in Paris.

Built in just 3 years (compared with nearly 200 for Notre Dame), Sainte Chapelle was consecrated in 1248. The chapel was conceived by Louis IX (St Louis) to house his collection of holy relics, including the alleged Crown of Thorns and part of John the Baptist's skull – for which he paid several times the cost of building the chapel itself. The relics were displayed on the wooden **canopied platform** in front of the altar, but the reliquary was destroyed during the Revolution and the relics relocated to Notre Dame.

Paris' oldest stained glass

On the right-hand side of the chapel, near the altar, is the **oratory**, where Louis would privately attend Mass without having to face his less-than-devout courtiers.

DON'T MISS
- 75m spire • evening medieval concerts
- statues of the apostles • window depicting the life of Moses

LA SEINE   (2, 3 & 5)

For most of Paris' 2000-year history the Seine was a major trade route, and the city's coat-of-arms still features the medieval boat motif of the Waterman's Guild. Today the river's islands, bridges and quays are Paris' most romantic attractions.

You can walk uninterrupted along the river's *quais* from **Pont Mirabeau** (2, G4) in the west to **Pont de Tolbiac** (2, J12) in the east; cycle the quais traffic-free on Sundays; or enjoy one of the many **riverboat cruises**. Whatever your preference, visit the Seine after nightfall, when it shimmers with the watery reflections of floodlit monuments and bridges.

The **Île de la Cité** (5, C5), the larger of the Seine's 2 linked islands, is the historic and tourist centre of Paris. **Notre Dame** is its prime attraction, but gorgeous **Sainte Chapelle**, the **Conciergerie**, the **flower market** and the moving **Mémorial des Martyrs de la Déportation** are all worth exploring.

Île St-Louis (5, D6), by contrast, has a village-like, provincial calm. The island's charming 17th-century stone houses, teahouses, boutiques and upmarket galleries provide a more reflective view of the city. The area around **Pont St-Louis** (linking the 2 islands) and **Pont Louis-Philippe** is quintessential picture-postcard Paris, and the city's best ice cream is sold at *Berthillon*, 31 rue St-Louis en l'Île.

Despite its name ('new bridge'), the **Pont Neuf** (5, A5; 1578-1604) is the oldest of the Seine's 37 bridges, and was once lined with houses and shops. Opposite the **Louvre**, the pedestrian-only **Pont des Arts** has outstanding views in both directions, while **Pont Alexandre III** (3, D5) is the most ornate and, some say, the most beautiful bridge in Paris.

Downstream, near the **Statue of Liberty** (2, G4), don't miss the modernist **Pont Mirabeau** with its wonderful evening views of the Tour Eiffel.

The walk on page 48 describes a stroll along the Seine.

A cruise boat passes under the Pont des Arts

DON'T MISS • Square du Vert Galant • Paris' newest bridge – the Passerelle Solférino • riverside bookstalls • Sunday cycling along the quais

TOUR EIFFEL   (3, F2)

It may have become the ubiquitous icon of mass tourism, but even the most jaded visitor is guaranteed to feel a frisson of excitement walking down the **Champ de Mars** towards the Tour Eiffel (Eiffel Tower).

By day, the tower is awesome: its massive size, its shape and its elemental construction make it as obvious a symbol of national potency today as when it was built to commemorate the centenary of the Revolution for the 1889 Exposition Universelle (World Fair).

At night, transformed by clever illumination, it floats on the edge of the Seine as if built of nothing more substantial than filaments of light.

Named for its designer, Gustave Eiffel, the tower reaches a height of 320m, including the television antenna at the very tip. This figure can vary by as much as 15cm, as the 7000-tonne tower of iron – held together by 2.5 million rivets – expands in warm weather and contracts when it's cold. It was the world's tallest structure until Manhattan's Chrysler Building was completed in 1930.

Almost torn down in 1909, the tower was spared for purely practical reasons – it proved an ideal platform for the transmitting antennas needed for the new science of radiotelegraphy.

When you're done peering upwards through the girders, take in the **panoramic views** from any of the 3 levels (at 57m, 115m and a heart-stopping 276m) open to the public. On a clear day (infrequent in Paris) the view from the top extends some 60km. If you're fit, you can avoid the lift queues by walking up the stairs in the south pillar to the 1st or 2nd platforms.

INFORMATION

- ✉ Champ de Mars, 7e
- ☎ 01 44 11 23 23
- Ⓜ Bir Hakeim; Trocadéro
- 🚆 RER Champ de Mars
- 🚌 42, 69, 72, 82, 87
- ⏱ 9.30am-11pm (mid-June-Aug 9am-midnight)
- ⑤ lift to 1st floor 21/12FF, 2nd floor 42/22FF and 3rd 60/31FF; stairway to 1st/2nd floors 15FF
- 🌐 www.tour-eiffel.fr
- ♿ limited
- 🍴 1st floor: cafe and Altitude 95 restaurant; 2nd floor: Jules Verne restaurant

Diana Mayfield

Rod Hyett

The view up the Tour Eiffel

DON'T MISS
- views at dusk • post office on the 2nd level
- Gustave Eiffel's 3rd-floor office • picnic in the Champ de Mars

sights & activities

Unlike many cities, Paris doesn't really have a 'centre' or 'downtown'. Parisian life is organised around *quartiers*, neighbourhoods with a particular identity or flavour; discovering the different essence of each quartier is one of the great delights of a visit to Paris.

Some of the oldest and most interesting quartiers – as well as many of the major monuments and sights – are strung along the banks of the Seine, between Pont de Sully in the east and Pont de la Concorde in the west, taking in the 1er, 4e, 5e and 6e *arrondissements*. You could easily spend weeks exploring this fascinating 3km stretch along the river.

The Islands
While their romantic beauty and monuments make them a natural magnet for visitors, locals rarely venture onto either of the Seine's 2 islands, except to cross from one side of the river to the other. Other than a handful of skating daredevils and the odd lovestruck couple, the **Île de la Cité** is almost deserted once the tourist buses depart. The **Île St-Louis** fares a little better because of its local population, but it's pretty sleepy after 9pm.

The Right Bank
The Right Bank is where it's all happening: in the last decade the former working-class areas of the Marais and Bastille (and Ménilmontant and Belleville, further north-east) have become the epicentre of a renewed urban spirit in Paris, attracting a young and cosmopolitan population with their avant-garde galleries, theatres and boutiques, and legions of bars, cafes and eateries.

A visit to the medieval Marais is a must; with its narrow streets, impressive *hôtels particuliers*, museums, Jewish quarter, boutique shopping, gay nightclubs and cafe life, it's Paris condensed.

If it's traditional big-city bustle you're craving, head for the department stores and international brand names on rue de Rivoli, or the pedestrianised shopping area between Les Halles and the Centre Pompidou.

The chic end of town is a little further west – the Palais Royal, Place Vendôme, Opéra and Madeleine – where you can visit some of the most gorgeous boutiques on earth and drink some of the most expensively wicked hot chocolate.

The Left Bank
While the Left Bank continues to harbour intellectuals and leftists, English is now the first language at the tacky end of blvd St-Michel and overwrought tourists have replaced highly strung artists and writers in St-Germain's Café Flore and Deux Magots.

But life still exists on the Left Bank: you'll find all manner of bookshops, cinemas and cafes in the narrow streets of the Quartier Latin and Mont Ste-Geneviève. In recent years the area around St-Sulpice has become a chic shopping neighbourhood, and close by there's Odéon, with its cinemas, cafes, clubs, crowds and collectibles.

MUSEUMS & GALLERIES

From the *Mona Lisa* to fake Cartier watches, Paris has museums to suit every passion – many housed in buildings at least as interesting as the collections themselves. Those listed here all have permanent collections; *Pariscope* and *L'Officiel des Spectacles* list temporary and travelling exhibitions.

Espace Montmartre Salvador Dalí (4, C5)
Over 300 works by Salvador Dalí (1904-89), the flamboyant Catalan surrealist printmaker, painter, sculptor and self-promoter, are on display at this museum around the corner from Place du Tertre.
✉ 9-11 rue Poulbot, 14e ☎ 01 42 64 40 10
Ⓜ Abbesses 🚍 64, 80
🕐 10am-6.30pm
⑤ 35/25FF ♿ limited

Fondation Cartier pour l'Art Contemporain (2, H9)
Brought to you by the designer watch and jewellery people, this conceptual gallery and performance space showcases contemporary art, design and installations; the stunningly modern HQ digs are by designer-architect Jean Nouvel (of Institut du Monde Arabe fame) with designer garden by Lothar Baumgarten.
✉ 261 blvd Raspail, 6e ☎ 01 53 67 40 00
🌐 www.fondation.cartier.fr Ⓜ Raspail
🚍 38, 68, 91 🕐 12-8pm; Nomad Soirée (live performance) Thurs 8.30pm
⑤ 30/20FF ♿ OK

Maison Européenne de la Photographie (5, D7)
The Maison Européenne de la Photographie, housed in an 18th-century hôtel partic-

Espace Montmartre Salvador Dalí

ulier, has permanent and temporary exhibits, an excellent Polaroid gallery, and a permanent homage to Irving Penn.
✉ 5-7 rue de Fourcy, 4e ☎ 01 44 78 75 00
🌐 www.mep-fr.org
Ⓜ St-Paul; Pont Marie
🚍 67, 69, 96, 76
🕐 Wed-Sun 11am-8pm
⑤ 30/15FF ♿ OK; magnifier for sight-impaired ✗ cafe

Musée Carnavalet-Musée de l'Histoire de Paris (5, D8)
Worth visiting for the 2 charming hôtels particuliers in which it's housed alone, this compelling museum illuminates the history of Paris from the Gallo-Roman period to the 20th century. Noteworthy exhibits include the keys to the Bastille, Napoleon's cradle and Proust's cork-lined bedroom.
✉ 23 rue de Sévigné, 3e ☎ 01 42 72 21 13
Ⓜ St-Paul; Chemin Vert
🚍 29, 69, 76, 96
🕐 Tues-Sun 10am-5.40pm ⑤ 35/25FF
♿ limited

Musée d'Art et d'Histoire du Judaisme (5, B8)
Recently inaugurated in a 17th-century mansion in the heart of the Marais, this museum recounts the history and everyday reality of Judaism, especially in France. Includes documents on the Dreyfus Affair and works by Chagall and Modigliani.
✉ Hôtel de St-Aignan, 71 rue du Temple, 3e
☎ 01 42 57 84 15
Ⓜ Arts et Métiers
🕐 Mon-Fri 11am-6pm, Sun 10am-6pm
⑤ 40/25FF ♿ OK

Musée d'Art Moderne de la Ville de Paris (3, D3)
If you like skateboarding and big art, the Palais de Tokyo is your kind of gallery. Dufy's *Fée Électricité* is said to be the world's biggest picture; *La Danse* by Matisse isn't far behind. You'll also find fauvism, cubism, surrealism and abstraction in abundance.
✉ 11 ave du Président Wilson, 16e ☎ 01 53

67 40 00 **Ⓜ Iéna;
Alma-Marceau 🚌 42,
63, 72, 80, 92** ⏰ Tues-
Fri 10am-5.30pm, Sat-
Sun 10am-6.45pm
⑤ 30/20FF
& OK

Musée d'Art Naïf Max Fourny (4, D7)

The vivid paintings in the Museum of Naive Art, gathered from around the world, have an immediate appeal, thanks in part to their whimsical and generally optimistic perspective on life.
✉ **Halle St-Pierre,
2 rue Ronsard, 18e**
☎ **01 42 58 72 89** ℮
www.hallestpierre.org
**Ⓜ Anvers 🚌 30, 54,
84** ⏰ 10am-6pm ⑤
40/30/20FF & limited

Musée de l'Armée

(3, F5) Everything you wanted to know about warfare but were afraid to ask, from Stone Age stick-throwing to WWI mustard gas. There's perhaps a few too many weapons, flags and medals, but Vizier, Napoleon's stuffed horse, is a crowd-pleaser.
✉ **Hôtel National des
Invalides, 129 rue de**

Grenelle, 7e
☎ **01 44 42 37 72**
℮ **www.invalides.org**
**Ⓜ La Tour Maubourg
🚌 24, 63, 67, 86, 87,
89** ⏰ summer 10am-
6pm, winter 10am-5pm
⑤ 38/28FF & OK

Musée de l'Homme

(3, E1) If you've never been to Easter Island, you can find one of those colossal heads in the Museum of Mankind. Fascinating exhibits cover human evolution, anthropology and culture over the past 3½ million years or so. Housed in the Palais de Chaillot, the museum has exhibits from Africa, Asia, Europe, the Arctic, the Pacific and the Americas.
✉ **Palais de Chaillot,
17 Place du Trocadéro,
16e** ☎ **01 44 05 72 72**
℮ **www.mnhn.fr**
**Ⓜ Trocadéro 🚌 22, 30,
32, 63, 72, 82** ⏰ Wed-
Mon 9.45am-7.15pm
⑤ 30/20/10FF & OK

Musée de l'Orangerie (3, D7)

The collection of 144 so-so impressionist works is eclipsed by Monet's astonishing *Water Lilies* – 8

huge panels conceived for the oval basement rooms of this former Tuileries greenhouse. The museum is undergoing renovations, and is due to reopen in 2001.
✉ **Jardin des Tuileries,
1er** ☎ **01 42 97 48 16**
**Ⓜ Concorde 🚌 24, 42,
52, 72, 73, 84, 94**
⏰ Wed-Mon 9.45am-
5.15pm ⑤ 30/20FF
& OK

Musée de la Curiosité et de la Magie (5, E7)

A delightful museum for kids of all ages interested in the ancient arts of magic, optical illusions and sleight of hand. Located in the *caves* of the house of the Marquis de Sade. Magic show included in the entry price.
✉ **11 rue St-Paul, 4e**
☎ **01 42 72 13 26**
**Ⓜ St-Paul 🚌 67, 69,
76, 96** ⏰ Wed & Sat-
Sun 2-7pm ⑤ 45/30FF
& no

Musée de la Mode et du Textile (3, D9)

This is a fascinating and envy-inspiring history of what Paris does best – fabrics, clothing and accessories from the 18th century to Dior, Schiaparelli and Paco Rabanne. More than 200,000 fashion images complement the exhibits.
✉ **Palais du Louvre,
107 rue de Rivoli, 1er**
☎ **01 44 55 57 50**
℮ **www.ucad.fr**
**Ⓜ Palais Royal
🚌 21, 27, 39, 48, 68,
69, 72, 81, 95** ⏰ Tues-
Fri 11am-6pm (Wed to
9pm), Sat-Sun 10am-
6pm ⑤ 35/25FF (incl
Musée des Arts
Décoratifs) & OK

Musée de la Monnaie

Martin Moos

Musée de la Monnaie (5, A4)

If you like your money old, spend some time in the former national mint (built 1770), which displays coins and medals from antiquity to the present as well as presses and other minting equipment.

✉ 11 Quai de Conti, 6e ☎ 01 40 46 55 35 **e** www.monnaiede paris.fr **M** Pont Neuf 🚌 27, 58, 70 ⏰ Tues-Fri 11am-5.30pm, Sat-Sun 12-5.30pm; mint tours Wed & Fri 2.15pm 💲 20/15FF; free Sun ♿ limited

Musée de la Serrure-Bricard (5, D8)

The Lock Museum showcases locks, keys and door knockers from ancient to modern times. Security conscious? Check out the lock that traps your hand in the jaws of a bronze lion if you insert the wrong key.

✉ 1 rue de la Perle, 3e ☎ 01 42 77 79 62 **M** St-Paul; Chemin Vert 🚌 29 ⏰ Mon-Fri 2-5pm 💲 30/15FF ♿ limited

Musée des Arts d'Afrique et d'Océanie (2, H15)

This unusual museum has something for everyone – incredibly expressive African tribal art, Australian Aboriginal art, colonial architecture, Art Deco furnishings – and an aquarium full of tropical fish and crocodiles in the basement!

✉ 293 ave Daumesnil, 12e ☎ 01 43 46 51 61 **M** Porte Dorée 🚌 46 ⏰ Wed-Mon 10am-5.30pm 💲 30/20FF ♿ limited

Musée des Arts Décoratifs (3, D9)

Rich, diverse collection of furniture, furnishings, jewellery and *objets d'art* (such as ceramics and glassware) from the Middle Ages and the Renaissance through to the Art Nouveau and Art Deco periods. The museum will be partly closed until 2001 due to Louvre renovations.

✉ Palais du Louvre, 107 rue de Rivoli, 1er ☎ 01 44 55 57 50 **e** www.ucad.fr **M** Palais Royal 🚌 21, 27, 39, 48, 68, 69, 72, 81, 95 ⏰ Tues-Sun 11am-6pm (Wed to 9pm), Sat-Sun 10am-6pm 💲 35/25FF (incl Musée de la Mode et du Textile) ♿ OK

Musée des Arts et Métiers (5, A9)

A compelling history of machines and instruments for anyone with a scientific bent. In pride of place is Foucault's original pendulum, which he introduced to the world with the words, 'Come and see the world turn'.

✉ 60 rue Réamur, 3e ☎ 01 40 27 23 31 **e** www.cnam.fr/museum **M** Arts et Métiers 🚌 21, 27, 38, 39, 47 ⏰ Tues-Sun10am-6pm, Thurs to 9.30pm 💲 35/25FF ♿ OK

Musée Edith Piaf (2, E12)

Die-hard fans of *la môme piaf* (the urchin sparrow) won't regret a thing about a visit to this tiny little museum in the working-class district of Belleville where she was born and began her career. Packed with memorabilia and lovingly tended; visits by prior appointment only.

✉ 5 rue Crespin du Gast, 11e ☎ 01 43 55 52 72 **M** Ménilmontant 🚌 96 ⏰ Mon-Thurs 1-6pm 💲 donation ♿ no

Musée Guimet/ Musée des Arts Asiatiques (3, D2)

Europe's most outstanding museum of Asian treasures includes sublime pieces from former French Indochina. If the massive renovations are still under way, you can content yourself with Emile Guimet's original collection of Chinese and Japanese Buddhas in the nearby Musée du Panthéon Bouddhique.

✉ 6 Place d'Iéna, 19 ave d'Iéna, 16e ☎ 01 45 05 00 98 **M** Iéna 🚌 22, 30, 32, 63, 82 ⏰ Wed-Sun 9.45am-6pm 💲 16/12FF ♿ no

Musée Gustave Moreau (2, C9)

Housed in the symbolist artist's former apartment and studio (complete with gorgeous spiral staircase), this quirky museum is crammed with thousands of paintings, drawings and sketches of Moreau's (1826-1898) favourite mythological and fantastic subjects.

✉ 14 rue de La Rochefoucauld, 9e ☎ 01 48 74 38 50 **M** Trinité 🚌 26, 32, 43, 68, 81 ⏰ Mon & Wed 11am-5.15pm, Thurs-Sun 10am-12.45pm & 2-5.15pm 💲 22/15FF ♿ limited

Musée Jacquemart-André

Musée Jacquemart-André (3, A5)

This enviable private art collection in an elegant townhouse is noted for its paintings by Rembrandt and Van Dyck, and the Italian Renaissance works of Bernini, Botticelli, Carpaccio, Donatello, Mantegna, Tintoretto, Titian and Uccello. The free audioguide explains the collection in detail.

✉ **158 blvd Haussmann, 8e** ☎ **01 42 89 04 91** Ⓜ **St-Philippe du Roule** 🚌 **22, 28, 43, 52, 54, 80, 83, 84, 93** ⏲ **10am-6pm** 💲 **48/36FF** ♿ **OK**

Musée Marmottan-Claude Monet (2, E3)

The Marmottan-Claude Monet Museum has not only the world's largest collection of works by the impressionist Claude Monet – including *Impression Soleil Levant* (which gave the impressionists their name) and a magnificent water-lily series – but also the exquisite Wildenstein illuminated manuscripts from the 13th century, major impressionist pieces and paintings by Gauguin and Renoir.

✉ **2 rue Louis-Boilly, 16e** ☎ **01 42 24 07 02** @ **www.marmottan .com** Ⓜ **La Muette** 🚌 **22, 32, 52** ⏲ **Tues-Sun 10am-5.30pm** 💲 **40/25FF** ♿ **OK**

Musée National des Arts et Traditions Populaires (2, C3)

The National Museum of Popular Arts and Traditions has displays illustrating life in rural France before and during the Industrial Revolution. If you've had a surfeit of kings, emperors and hôtels particuliers, the antidote is this view of how the other half – the rural poor – lived, worked and played in pre-industrial France.

✉ **6 ave du Mahatma Gandhi, 16e** ☎ **01 44 17 60 00** @ **www .culture.fr/culture/atp /mnatp** Ⓜ **Les Sablons** 🚌 **73, 244** ⏲ **Wed-Mon 9.30am-5.15pm** 💲 **25/17FF** ♿ **OK**

Musée National du Moyen Âge-Thermes de Cluny (5, C4)

One of the world's finest collections of medieval statuary, illuminated manuscripts and arts & crafts, housed in **Gallo-Roman baths** dating from around AD 200 and the late 15th-century **Hôtel de Cluny** – the finest example of medieval civil architecture in Paris.

✉ **6 Place Paul Painlevé, 5e** ☎ **01 53 73 78 00** Ⓜ **Cluny La Sorbonne** 🚌 **21, 27, 38, 63, 85, 86, 87** ⏲ **Wed-Mon 9.15am-5.45pm** 💲 **30/20FF** ♿ **limited**

Musée National Eugène Delacroix (3, G9)

Delacroix, leader of the romantic school of painting, moved to this apartment/studio while he painted the murals in nearby Église St-Sulpice, and he remained here until his death in 1863. You'll see some minor works, sketches and the artist's personal mementoes.

✉ **6 Place de Furstemberg, 6e** ☎ **01 44 41 86 50** Ⓜ **Mabillon; St-Germain des Prés** 🚌 **39, 48, 63, 95** ⏲ **Wed-Mon 9.30am-5.30pm** 💲 **22/15FF** ♿ **limited**

Musée National Eugène Delacroix

NOTABLE BUILDINGS

Paris is full of majestic old buildings, and some pretty impressive new ones as well. Here's a few that are worth having a look at in between cafes.

Bibliothèque Nationale de France François Mitterrand

(2, H12) The National Library has more than 10 million books and historical documents shelved in its 4 strikingly modern 80m-high towers, resembling open books.

✉ 11 Quai François Mauriac, 13e ☎ 01 53 79 49 49 ℮ www.bnf.fr Ⓜ Quai de la Gare 🚌 62, 89 ⏰ Tues-Sat 10am-8pm, Sun 12-7pm ⑤ free ♿ OK

Conciergerie (5, B5)

The fairy-tale Conciergerie building was a royal palace in the 14th century, before becoming a prison, torture chamber and lock-up for nearly 3000 victims of the guillotine. The **Tour de l'Horloge** houses Paris' first public clock (1370).

✉ 1 Quai de l'Horloge, 1er ☎ 01 53 73 78 50 Ⓜ Cité 🚌 21, 24, 27, 38, 58, 81, 85 ⏰ summer 9.30am-6.30pm, winter 10am-5pm ⑤ 35/23FF ♿ limited

Hôtel de Sully (5, E7)

The Hôtel de Sully is a superb, early 17th-century aristocratic mansion. The late Renaissance-style courtyards are adorned with bas-reliefs of the seasons and the elements. Temporary photographic exhibitions are held in the orangerie.

✉ 62 rue St-Antoine, 4e ☎ 01 44 61 20 00

Ⓜ St-Paul 🚌 20, 29, 61, 65, 69, 76, 86, 87, 91 ⏰ garden 9am-7pm; info centre and library Tues-Sat 10am-6pm ⑤ free; fee for exhibitions ♿ limited

Hôtel de Ville (5, C6)

Paris' city hall was rebuilt in the neo-Renaissance style between 1874 and 1882 after having been gutted during the Paris Commune (1871). The ornate façade is decorated with 108 statues of noteworthy Parisians.

✉ Place de l'Hôtel de Ville, 4e ☎ 01 42 76 50 49 ℮ www.parisfrance.org Ⓜ Hôtel de Ville 🚌 21, 27, 38, 85, 96 ⑤ free tours (in French) first Mon of the month at 10.30am ♿ limited

Institut du Monde Arabe (5, E5)

The striking façade has thousands of aperture-like windows which regulate light and heat. On the 7th floor is a museum of 9th to 19th-century art and artisanship from all over the Arab world, while the teahouse on the 9th floor has great views.

✉ 1 rue des Fossés St-Bernard, 5e ☎ 01 40 51 38 38 ℮ www.imarabe.org Ⓜ Cardinal Lemoine; Jussieu 🚌 24, 63, 67, 86, 87, 89 ⏰ Tues-Sun 10am-6pm ⑤ building free; museum 25/20FF ♿ OK

Opéra Bastille

(3, G15) Inaugurated on the 200th anniversary of the storming of the Bastille, Paris' high-tech 'second' opera house has weathered political fallout and technical problems to become a concert favourite.

✉ 2-6 Place de la Bastille, 11e ☎ 01 40 01 19 70 ℮ www.opera-de-paris.fr Ⓜ Bastille 🚌 20, 29, 65, 69, 76, 86, 87, 91 ⏰ guided tours daily ⑤ 54/30FF ♿ OK

Opéra Garnier (3, B9)

Now home to ballet rather than opera, this grandiose theatre was designed by 35-year-old Charles Garnier to trumpet Napoleon III's Second Empire. Chagall redecorated the auditorium ceiling in 1964.

✉ Place de l'Opéra, 9e ☎ 01 40 01 22 63 ℮ www.opera-de-paris.fr Ⓜ Opéra 🚌 20, 21, 22, 27, 29, 31, 39, 42,

Rob Flynn

Institut du Monde Arabe

Statues & Monuments

The French immortalise their heroes with statues and monuments. The cemeteries – Père Lachaise, Montmartre, Montparnasse – are bursting with wonderfully evocative likenesses of heroes and villains, poets and philosophers, revolutionaries and autocrats; and there's a resident stone or bronze celebrity in even the tiniest park.

Here's a selection of the larger-than-life personalities you might bump into on your way around Paris:

Saint Denis, patron saint of France, introduced Christianity to Paris and was beheaded by the Romans for his pains. You can see him carrying his head under his arm on the portal of Notre Dame (5, C5).

Sainte Geneviève, patron saint of Paris, turned Attila the Hun away from Paris in 451. Now she stands, ghostly pale, turning her back on the city from high above the Pont de la Tournelle on Île St-Louis (5, E5). A millennium later, spunky **Jeanne d'Arc** (Joan of Arc) tried unsuccessfully to wrest Paris from the English in 1429; her gilded likeness now stands in the Place des Pyramides (3, D9), not far from where she was wounded.

Henri IV, known as the Vert Galant ('jolly rogue' or 'dirty old man' depending on your perspective), sits astride his horse on the Pont Neuf (5, A5), looking very vert indeed. **Charlemagne**, emperor of the Francs, rides his steed under the trees in front of Notre Dame (5, C5), while a poor imitation of the

Henry IV, Vert Galant

Sun King, **Louis XIV**, prances in the Place des Victoires (3, D10). **Napoleon**, horseless and in drag, stands atop the column in Place Vendôme (3, C8).

But it's not all saints and kings. **Georges Danton**, a leader (and later victim) of the Revolution, stands reunited with his head near the site of his house at Odéon (5, B3). A tackily lit bronze replica of the **Statue of Liberty** – recently returned from a year in Tokyo Harbour – faces New York from the artificial island Allée des Cygnes (Swan's Walk; 2, G4).

The **Liberty Flame**, near the Pont de l'Alma (3, D3), was erected as a tribute to the Résistance fighters of WWII, but has become a de facto memorial to Diana, Princess of Wales, whose chauffeur-driven car failed to exit the nearby tunnel; it's littered with heart-felt notes scrawled in a dozen languages.

52, 53, 66, 68, 81 ⊙ summer 10am-6pm, winter 10am-5pm ⑤ 30/20FF ♿ limited

Palais de Chaillot

(3, D1) The distinctive curved, colonnaded wings of the *palais*, built for the World Exhibition of 1937, house 4 museums – including the Musée de l'Homme. The terrace has an exceptional panorama of the Jardins du Trocadéro, the Seine and the Tour Eiffel.

✉ Place du Trocadéro, 16e Ⓜ Trocadéro ☒ 22, 30, 32, 63, 72, 82 ⊙ 9.45am-5.15pm ♿ OK

Panthéon (5, D3)

The Panthéon's dome dominates the Quartier Latin. Inside are the mortal remains of 62 'great men', including Voltaire, Rousseau, Louis Braille, Victor Hugo, Émile Zola … and Marie Curie.

✉ Place du Panthéon, 5e ☎ 01 44 32 18 00 Ⓜ Cardinal Lemoine ☒ 84, 89 ⊙ summer 9.30am-6.30pm, winter 10am-6.15pm ⑤ 30/25FF ♿ no

Tour de Jean Sans Peur (3, D11)

The 6-floor, 29m Gothic tower of 'John without fear' was built by the Duc de Bourogne in the early 15th century so he could hide at the top, safe from his enemies. It has recently opened to visitors.

✉ 20 rue Étienne Marcel, 2e ☎ 01 42 61 55 02 Ⓜ Étienne Marcel ⊙ Thurs, Sat & Sun (Tues-Sun during school vacations) 1.30-8pm ⑤ 30FF/20FF ♿ no

PLACES & SPACES

Postcard visions of Paris are often constructed around pretty little *places* (squares), lined with cafe tables where happy imbibers quaff wine in the spring sunshine. There are dozens of these smaller *places*, such as the **Place du Marché Ste-Catherine** (5, E7) in the Marais district, but the larger squares are equally impressive.

Place de Furstemberg
(5, A3) Tucked in behind St-Germain des Prés, this tiny little square takes on a special life on summer evenings, when magnolias perfume the air and buskers serenade lovers under the old-fashioned streetlamp.
✉ **Place de Furstemberg, 6e Ⓜ St-Germain des Prés** 🚌 **39, 48, 63, 70, 86, 87, 95, 96**

Place de l'Hôtel de Ville (5, C6)
The **Hôtel de Ville** (city hall) faces this fountain-and-lamp-adorned square, since the Middle Ages the venue for many of Paris' celebrations, rebellions, book burnings and public executions. In winter the square is adorned with a dinky ice-skating rink.
✉ **Place de l'Hôtel de Ville, 1er Ⓜ Hôtel de Ville** 🚌 **67, 86, 87**

Place de la Bastille
(3, G15) The prison has gone, but the mobs remain – mostly heading to the trendy bars and restaurants nearby. In the centre, gilded Liberty perches atop the **Colonne de Juillet** (July Column), a memorial to the revolutions of 1830 and 1848.
✉ **Place de la Bastille, 11e Ⓜ Bastille**

Place de la Concorde
(3, D7) Louis XVI was guillotined here in 1793, followed by another 1343

victims over the next 2 years. Renamed following the Reign of Terror, it's now the world's most chaotic traffic roundabout, with impressive vistas from the 3300-year-old Egyptian obelisk at its centre.
✉ **Place de la Concorde, 8e Ⓜ Concorde** 🚌 **24, 42, 52, 72, 73, 84, 94**

Place de la Contrescarpe (5, E3)
This convivial little square in the Quartier Latin, frequented by students, is a great place for a quick lunch or an *apéritif* before heading off to one of the dozens of inexpensive restaurants nearby.
✉ **Place de la Contrescarpe, 5e Ⓜ Place Monge** 🚌 **47**

Place des Abbesses
(4, D5) This bustling little square is a far better place to sample the 'village' life of Montmartre than tourist-trap Place du Tertre. Don't miss the original

Hector Guimard Art Nouveau metro entrance, one of only 2 surviving.
✉ **Place des Abbesses, 18e Ⓜ Abbesses** 🚌 **30, 31, 54, 56, 67, 80, 85, 95**

Place des Victoires
(3, D10) Designed for Louis XIV by the architect of Versailles, this charming and intimate 'square', surrounded by a ring of elegant 17th-century buildings, is now home to the designer labels Kenzo, Victoire and Mugler.
✉ **Place des Victoires, 1er, 2e Ⓜ Sentier** 🚌 **29, 48, 67, 74**

Place Vendôme
(3, C8) Austere, pompous and beautiful, octagonal Place Vendôme and the arcaded and colonnaded buildings around it epitomise Parisian wealth and privilege. Napoleon married Josephine at No 3, and Di and Dodi took the Merc for a final spin from the **Hôtel Ritz**.
✉ **Place Vendôme, 1er Ⓜ Tuileries** 🚌 **72**

Cafe society, Place de la Bastille

Simon Bracken

PLACES OF WORSHIP

Paris' religious buildings are amongst the city's best loved attractions, offering respite from the crowds, with a little architectural history thrown in for good measure.

Église St-Étienne du Mont (5, E3)

The carved rood screen is the only one remaining in Paris. Relics of Sainte Geneviève (patron saint of Paris) are in the ambulatory, and a plaque on the floor marks the spot where a defrocked priest killed a bishop in 1857.

✉ Place Ste-Geneviève, 5e Ⓜ Cardinal Lemoine ☒ 84, 89 ⏲ Mon-Sat 8am-7pm, Sun 9am-7pm Ⓢ free ♿ OK

Église St-Eustache

(3, D11) Louis XIV celebrated his first communion in this beautiful church, a mixture of Gothic design and Renaissance decoration. Liszt and Berlioz both premiered new works here, and the church is still renowned for its choral and organ music.

✉ Place du Jour, 1er Ⓜ Les Halles ☒ 29, 38, 47, 74 ⏲ Mon-Sat 9am-7pm, Sun 8.15am-12.30pm & 2.30-7pm; Mass with Gregorian chant Sun 11am Ⓢ free ♿ OK

Église St-Germain des Prés (5, A3)

The oldest church in Paris is not, unfortunately, the most interesting. The ghostly bell tower over the west entrance is probably around 1000 years old, though the spire was added much later. St-Symphorian chapel contains the tomb of Saint Germanus (died 576).

✉ Place St-Germain des Prés, 6e Ⓜ St-Germain des Prés ☒ 39, 48, 63, 70, 86, 87, 95, 96 ⏲ Mon-Sat 8am-7.45pm, Sun 9am-8pm Ⓢ free ♿ OK

Église St-Séverin

(5, C4) A gem of flamboyant Gothic architecture – especially in the spiralling stonework of the ambulatory – St-Séverin was built in one of the oldest quarters of Paris between the 13th and 16th centuries. Today it's a favourite subject of local artists.

✉ 1 rue des Prêtres-St-Séverin, 5e Ⓜ St-Michel ☒ 21, 24, 27, 38, 85, 96 ⏲ Mon-Sat 11am-

7.30pm, Sun 9am-8.30pm Ⓢ free ♿ OK

Église St-Sulpice

(5, B2) Delacroix's vivid murals – *St Michael Killing the Demon* and *Jacob Wrestling the Angel* – are highlights of this richly decorated 17th-century church with its unusual Italianate façade.

✉ Place St-Sulpice, 6e Ⓜ St-Sulpice ☒ 63, 70, 84, 86, 87, 96 ⏲ 7.30am-7.30pm; Mass with Gregorian chant Sun 10.30am Ⓢ free ♿ OK

Guimard Synagogue

(5, D7) While Paris has a number of synagogues, the one in Paris' first paved street has a façade designed by Art Nouveau doyen Hector Guimard, best known for his playful Metro entrances.

✉ 8 rue Pavée, 4e ☎ 01 48 87 21 54 Ⓜ St-Paul ☒ 67, 69, 96, 76 ⏲ not open to the public

Mosquée de Paris

(3, K13) An exotic slice of the Maghreb in the heart of the Quartier Latin. Built in the ornate Hispano-Moorish style, with serene, decorated courtyards and pink-marble fountains, plus an African-style *salon de thé* and *hammam* (bathhouse).

✉ Place du Puits-de-l'Ermite, 5e ☎ 01 45 35 97 33 Ⓜ Place Monge ☒ 63, 67, 86, 87, 89 Ⓢ donation ♿ OK

Tranquil courtyard in the Mosquée de Paris

Simon Bracken

PARKS & PROMENADES

There may be over 90,000 trees (mostly plane and chestnut) in Paris, but at times the city can feel chokingly urban. Fortunately, there are more than 400 parks to choose from – some the size of a handkerchief, others the size of a small village.

Bois de Boulogne
(2, E2) These huge Haussmann-designed woods on the western edge of the city boast lakes, lawns, forests, flower gardens, meandering paths, cycling trails and *belle époque* cafes. Have a picnic, hire a bike or rowing boat, or stroll through the beautiful Parc de Bagatelle (2, D2).
Ⓜ **Porte Dauphine; Porte Maillot; Porte d'Auteuil** 🚌 **43, 52, 63, 73, 82** 🕐 **24hrs (avoid after dark)** Ⓢ **free** ♿ **OK**

Bois de Vincennes
(2, J15) These vast, well-ordered gardens east of the city have 3 lakes, a zoo, floral and tropical gardens, a Buddhist centre and bike paths. The Foire du Trône amusement park (Apr-May) and turreted, medieval Château de Vincennes are also worth a look.
☎ **01 48 08 31 20** Ⓜ **Château de Vincennes** 🚆 **RER Nogent-sur-Marne** 🚌 **325, 56** 🕐 **park dawn-dusk; château 10am-5pm (summer to 6pm)** Ⓢ **park free; château 32/21FF** ♿ **OK**

Cimetière du Montparnasse (3, K8)
This tranquil little cemetery contains the tombs of such illustrious personages as Charles Baudelaire, Samuel Beckett, Guy de

Not your average park fence

Maupassant, Simone de Beauvoir and Jean-Paul Sartre, André Citroën, Alfred Dreyfus, Jean Seberg, Serge Gainsbourg and Man Ray. Don't miss Constantin Brancusi's intriguing sculpture *The Kiss*.
✉ **Conservation office, 3 blvd Edgar Quinet, 14e** ☎ **01 44 10 86 50** Ⓜ **Edgar Quinet; Raspail** 🚌 **54, 80, 95, 320** 🕐 **Mon-Fri 8am-6pm (winter to 5.30pm), Sat from 8.30am, Sun from 9am** Ⓢ **free** ♿ **limited**

Jardin des Plantes
(3, J14) Founded in 1626 as a medicinal herb garden for Louis XIII, Paris' botanical gardens are endearingly informal, even unkempt. There are several greenhouses, a small *ménagerie* and the

fascinating Grande Galerie de l'Evolution, part of the Musée National d'Histoire Naturelle.
✉ **57 rue Cuvier, 5e** ☎ **01 40 79 34 00** 🖥 **www.mnhn.fr** Ⓜ **Gare d'Austerlitz; Jussieu** 🚌 **24, 61, 63, 65, 67, 89, 91** 🕐 **park dawn-dusk; galerie Mon & Wed-Fri 1-5pm** Ⓢ **galerie 15/10FF** ♿ **limited**

Jardin des Tuileries
(3, D8) Once the most fashionable strolling park in Paris, the formal Tuileries offers respite from the crowds, plus all those views of great monuments. Kids can float boats in the pond, and twice a year there's a carnival with heart-stopping Ferris-wheel rides.
☎ **01 40 20 90 43** Ⓜ **Tuileries; Concorde**

Artist, Jardin des Tuileries

Spring has sprung – the best time to visit Paris' gardens

🚌 21, 27, 39, 48, 68, 69, 72, 81, 95 ⊙ dawn-dusk ⑤ free ♿ OK

Parc André Citroën
(2, H4) Built on the banks of the Seine on the 14-hectare former Citroën manufacturing plant, this high-tech architect-designed park is a series of thematic 'spaces' – the 'white garden', the 'black garden' and the whimsical 'restless garden'.
✉ rue Balard, 15e Ⓜ Balard 🚌 42 ⊙ dawn-dusk ♿ OK

Parc de Monceau
(2, C7) The dauntingly pretty Parc de Monceau is surrounded by the chic and expensive apartments of the *haute bourgeoisie*, and has immaculately tended lawns, pseudo-classical statuary and the city's best-dressed kids out with their nannies.
✉ blvd de Courcelles, 8e Ⓜ Monceau 🚌 30, 84, 94 ⊙ dawn-dusk ♿ OK

Parc des Buttes Chaumont (2, C13)
A slice of Manhattan's Central Park in the northeast of Paris, this former quarry is now a lush, hilly landscape with a huge lake, forested slopes, hidden grottoes, artificial waterfalls and views of Montmartre. A good spot for jogging, tanning or hearing a bird.
✉ rue Armand Carrel, 19e ☎ 01 40 36 41 32 Ⓜ Buttes Chaumont; Botzaris 🚌 26, 60, 75 ⊙ 7am-9pm (summer to 11pm) ⑤ free ♿ limited

Promenade Plantée
(2, G12) For an elevated perspective over eastern Paris, follow the tree and flower-lined *coulée verte* (green strip) built atop the 4.5km viaduct that once carried trains between Bastille and the Bois de Vincennes. Below are the trendy shops and *ateliers* of the **Viaduc des Arts**.
✉ ave Daumesnil between Opéra Bastille and Porte Dorée, 12e ℮ www.promenade-plantee.org Ⓜ Bastille; Reuilly Diderot

Survivors of a tour of the Musée du Louvre recover in the nearby Jardin des Tuileries

PARIS FOR CHILDREN

Keeping children entertained on an endless round of museum and gallery visits can be difficult, but there are many other sights that both adults and kids will find enjoyable. Parc de la Villette offers endless possibilities.

Disneyland Paris (1, C9)

Not Disneyland-does-Paris but a replica of Disney amusement parks in Japan and the USA, with the usual assortment of rides, parades, cartoon characters and fattening foods. Disneyland Paris is 32km east of Paris.

✉ Marne-la-Vallé Cedex 4 ☎ 01 60 30 60 30 🌐 www.disney land.paris.com 🚉 RER to Marne-la-Vallé-Chessy (line A4) ⏰ Sept-June 10am-6pm, July-Aug 9am-11pm ⑤ Mar-Oct & Christmas holidays 220/170FF, Nov-Feb 165/135FF ♿ limited

Jardin d'Acclimation (2, C3)

This park, funfair and amusement park for the youngsters in the Bois de Boulogne has puppet shows, an enchanted-river boatride, a toy train, dodgems, mini-golf, donkey rides and a children's zoo.

✉ Bois de Boulogne, 16e ☎ 01 40 67 90 82 🚇 Les Sablons 🚌 43, 52, 63, 73, 82 ⏰ 10am-6pm ⑤ 10FF for some attractions ♿ limited

La Musée de la Poupée (5, B8)

A delightful little museum with more than 300 dolls (many of French porcelain) from 1840 to today, together with doll houses, accessories, miniature toys, and a doll hospital and shop.

✉ Impasse Berthaud (nr 22 rue Beaubourg), 3e ☎ 01 42 72 73 11 🚇 Rambuteau 🚌 29, 38, 47, 75 ⏰ Tues-Sun 10am-6pm ⑤ 35/25FF ♿ OK

Musée Grévin (3, B10)

This waxworks museum inside the Passage Jouffroy is not a patch on Madame Tussaud's, but would you get to see the death masks of French Revolutionary leaders in London? There's also a Magic Theatre and Hall of Mirrors from 1900.

✉ Passage Jouffroy, 10-12 blvd Montmartre, 9e ☎ 01 47 70 85 05 🌐 www.musee-grevin .com 🚇 Rue Montmartre 🚌 20, 48, 74, 85 ⏰ 1-7pm (from 10am school holidays) ⑤ 58/38FF ♿ limited

Palais de la Découverte (3, D5)

Tucked away in the Grand Palais, and usually full of earnest school groups, the Palace of Discovery has informative interactive exhibits on the sciences, from astronomy (including a state-of-the-art planetarium) to medicine.

✉ ave Franklin D Roosevelt, 8e ☎ 01 40 74 80 00 🌐 www.palais-decou verte.fr 🚇 Champs Élysées Clemenceau 🚌 28, 42, 49, 52, 63, 72, 73, 80, 83, 93

⏰ Tues-Sat 9.30am-6pm, Sun 10am-7pm; planetarium 11.30am, 2.15, 3.30 & 4.45pm ⑤ 27/17FF; planetarium 13FF ♿ limited

Parc Zoologique de Paris (2, J15)

The 1200 captives in France's largest zoo include all the usual exotic suspects, plus panda; the wild mountain sheep who live on the 70m-high artificial rock in the centre of the park seem to have the most fun. Summer weekends are usually crowded.

✉ 53 ave St-Maurice, 12e ☎ 01 44 75 20 1 🌐 www.mnhn.fr 🚇 Porte Dorée 🚌 46, 86, 325 ⏰ summer 9am-6pm (Sun to 6.30pm), winter 9am-5pm (Sun to 5.30pm) ⑤ 40/30/10FF ♿ OK

Babysitting

If you need a break from the kids, hire a babysitter. Ababa (☎ 01 45 49 15 86; 64FF agency fee plus 33FF/hr) and Pro-sitting (☎ 01 44 37 91 11; 45FF agency fee plus 33FF/hr) are both recommended. English-speaking students are sometimes available for childminding through Alliance Française (☎ 01 45 44 38 28).

QUIRKY PARIS

Paris is a very cosmopolitan city, so if you're looking for something a little off-beat this is your town. The colourful Marais district (p. 20) and the Cimetière du Père Lachaise (p. 16) are good places to start, but they're certainly not the end of things.

Brocante

A fun way to buy all manner of second-hand stuff is at an impromptu *brocante* (trash and treasure) market, often held along major thoroughfares in spring and autumn. Banners advertise locations a few days before the market begins.

Catacombes de Paris

(2, H9) From 1785, nearly 6 million skeletons were taken from Paris' overburdened cemeteries and neatly stacked in disused underground quarries, creating Paris' most macabre museum. During WWII, the tunnels were used as a headquarters by the Résistance.
✉ 1 Place Denfert

Musée de l'Érotisme

Rochereau, 14e ☎ 01 43 22 47 63 Ⓜ Denfert Rochereau 🚌 38, 68 ⊙ Tues-Fri 2-4pm, Sat-Sun 9-11am & 2-4pm ⓢ 27/19FF ♿ no

Colette's Water Bar

(3, D8) Sick of nursing a *gueule de bois* (hangover) the next day? At the 'water bar' in the basement of this chic shopping temple you can tipple 100 types of drinking water – both sparkling and still – from around the world.
✉ 213 rue St-Honoré, 1er ☎ 01 55 35 33 90 ② www.colette.tm.fr Ⓜ Tuileries 🚌 69, 72 ⊙ 10.30am-7.30pm ⓢ free ♿ limited

Hammam de la Mosquée de Paris

(3, K13) Step out of the west and into the east in this wonderfully exotic bathhouse at Paris' Grand Mosque. Relax in the public baths (men and women on different days) or experience a traditional massage. Finish with mint tea.
✉ 39 rue Geoffroy-St-Hilaire, 5e ☎ 01 43 31 18 14 Ⓜ Place Monge 🚌 69, 72 ⊙ 10am-9pm; men Tues & Sun, women other days ⓢ baths 85FF; massage 55FF ♿ limited

Musée de l'Érotisme

(4, D3) Pigalle's Museum of Eroticism tries to put titillating statuary and sexual aids from days gone by

on a loftier plane – with 7 floors of erotic art from 4 continents. But we all know why we've come.
✉ 72 blvd de Clichy, 18e ☎ 01 42 58 28 73 ② www.erotic-museum.com Ⓜ Blanche 🚌 30, 54, 74, 80, 95 ⊙ 10am-2am ⓢ 40/30FF ♿ limited

Musée des Égouts de Paris

(3, D4) Raw sewage complete with all sorts of vaguely familiar floating objects flows beneath your feet as you walk through 480m (of more than 2100km!) of odoriferous tunnels, passing artefacts illustrating the development of Paris' wastewater-disposal system.
✉ 93 Quai d'Orsay, 7e ☎ 01 53 68 27 81 Ⓜ Alma-Marceau 🚌 42, 63, 80, 92 ⊙ summer 11am-5pm, winter 11am-4pm ⓢ 25/20FF ♿ no

Pari Roller

(2, J10) Every Friday night more than 5000 skaters (record 28,000!) take to the streets for an officially sponsored 3hr, 25km frolic through the heart of the city. The route varies weekly, but often passes through Bastille around midnight.
✉ depart 40 ave d'Italie, 13e ② www.pari-roller.com Ⓜ Place d'Italie ⊙ Fri 10pm-1am ⓢ free ♿ no

OFF THE BEATEN TRACK

At times Paris seems gridlocked with tourists, but surprisingly you can quite literally turn two corners from Notre Dame or Sacré Cœur and not see another soul. Here's a few ideas for escaping the marauding hordes.

Belleville   (2, D12)

The neighbourhood around the Belleville metro is one of the most ethnically diverse in all of Paris, with West African, Arab, Greek, Turkish, Polish, Vietnamese and Chinese populations. It's a fascinating area to wander around while savouring the sights and smells – especially on market mornings (Tuesday and Friday).

La Butte aux Cailles   (2, J10)

Despite the encroaching apartment blocks, 'Quail Hill' has managed to retain a 19th-century village feel, thanks to its picturesque cobbled streets, old houses and bohemian cafes and restaurants. Wander along rue de la Buttes aux Cailles and rue des Cinq Diamantes, not forgetting to detour now and then. To get there, catch the metro to Place d'Italie or Corvisart.

Canal St-Martin   (2, D11)

The 4.5km-long Canal St-Martin is one of Paris' hidden delights. Its shaded towpaths – dappled with sunlight filtering through the plane trees – are a wonderful place for a romantic stroll or bike ride past 9 locks, lovely bridges and ordinary Parisian neighbourhoods. République or Jaurès metros will get you there.

Rob Flynn

Montsouris   (2, K9)

Canal St-Martin

After a picnic or stroll in lovely Parc Montsouris, explore the old-fashioned cottages and artists' studios in and south of cobbled Square de Montsouris. Revolutionaries Henry Miller, Salvador Dalí and Lenin lived (separately) in a bohemian enclave north of the Réservoirs de Montsouris; Miller celebrated his little cul-de-sac, Villa Seurat, as Villa Borghese in *Tropic of Cancer*. Catch the metro to Cité Universitaire.

Place Dauphine   (5, A5)

Nestled near the western end of the Île de la Cité is Paris' oldest square (commissioned by Henri IV), a surprisingly restful spot in the heart of the city. Pont Neuf is the closest metro.

Port de l'Arsenal (3, H15)

Hidden away just metres from the throbbing traffic roundabout at Bastille is Paris' working port. It's a pleasant place to stroll or have a picnic or *apéritif*, while watching the boats and barges come and go. There's a playground and sandpit for youngsters.

KEEPING FIT

It's not unusual to gain an extra kilo or 2 during a visit to Paris, no matter how many museum corridors you pound. **Allô-Sports** (☎ 01 42 76 54 54) is a useful helpline (English spoken) offering advice on sports and activities throughout Paris.

Climbing

To practise for your Alps freeclimb, there are 5 *murs d'escalade* located in the 14-19e. You'll need your own gear, proof of insurance, an ID photo and 20FF for a subscription. For more information call ☎ 01 42 51 24 68.

Cycling

Paris traffic is dangerous, so don't even think of renting a bike unless you're a confident big-city cyclist. Two of the best city rides away from the traffic are along the closed-to-traffic **river *quais*** on Sunday, and along the 50km **Canal St-Martin/Canal de l'Ourcq** route – traffic-free after Place de la Bataille de Stalingrad (2, C11). Otherwise, head for the relative safety of the **Bois du Boulogne** and **Bois de Vincennes**.

Making the most of Sunday's traffic-free quais

Golf

Although there are no golf courses in the city itself, there are a couple of practice ranges in Paris if you want to keep your swing limber. The **French Golf Federation** (☎ 01 41 49 77 00) can provide you with a list of public courses.

Gyms

It seems like everyone in Paris belongs to a gym, and on Saturday morning that's where you'll find them. Expensive temporary memberships or day passes are available at many, though facilities are often crowded at peak times.

Jogging

You rarely see joggers in Paris, partly because of the pollution and traffic, and partly because the style police frown on sweaty people in shorts. Best spots for an uninterrupted run in the city are the **Jardin du Luxembourg**, **Champ de Mars**, **Parc des Buttes Chaumont** or along the **Promenade Plantée**. Further afield, try the **Bois de Boulogne** and **Bois de Vincennes**.

Skating

Paris is relatively flat and paved throughout, so there are plenty of off-road opportunities for skaters – whether you prefer inline, roller or board. Ice skating is popular at outdoor rinks in winter.

Swimming

Paris has more than 30 pools open to the public – ask at your hotel for the nearest. Most are short-length pools and finding a free lane for laps is nigh on impossible. Opening times vary widely; avoid Wednesday afternoon and Saturday when school kids take the plunge.

Tennis & Squash

Demand greatly exceeds supply for tennis and squash courts, so book well ahead if you want a game.

Aquaboulevard
(2, J4) Huge recreational centre offering a range of activities for adults and kids, including swimming pool, 'beach' and aquatic park, tennis, squash, golf practice and gym, restaurants etc.
✉ 4 rue Louis-Armand, 15e ☎ 01 40 60 10 00
Ⓜ Balard ◷ 9am-midnight Ⓢ 70/58FF half-day entry

Dojo Zen de Paris
(2, J10) Perhaps not an activity to open up the sweat pores, but a session of *zazen* just might open your third eye. The dojo was founded by Taisen Deshimaru in 1971; free introductory zazen sessions are offered Sat at 4pm.
✉ 175 rue de Tolbiac, 13e ☎ 01 53 80 19 19
Ⓜ Tolbiac ◷ zazen Tues-Fri 6.30 & 7.30am, 12.30 & 7pm, Sat 11am
& 5pm, Sun 11am
Ⓢ 30FF per session, 230FF per month

Gymnase Club
Paris' biggest chain of gyms has over 20 locations in the city and good facilities (some including pools and sauna).
✉ 147 bis rue St-Honoré, 1er (3, E9)
☎ 01 40 20 03 03
Ⓜ Palais-Royal
ⓔ www.gymnaseclub.fr
◷ depends on location
Ⓢ depends on location

Paris à Vélo c'est Sympa (3, G15)
This centrally located bike-rental outlet also offers an interesting range of thematic bike tours, including 'Quirky Paris' and 'Paris by Night'.
✉ 37 blvd Bourdon, 4e
☎ 01 48 87 60 01
ⓔ www.parisvelo sympa.com Ⓜ Bastille
◷ 9am-noon & 2-7pm
Ⓢ 80/55FF full/half-day plus 2000FF deposit (credit card OK); tours 170/150FF

Piscine Pontoise
(5, E5) Beautiful Art Deco-style swimming pool (33m) in the heart of the Quartier Latin. Complex also includes gym and squash courts.
✉ 19 rue de Pontoise, 5e ☎ 01 43 54 82 45
Ⓜ Maubert Mutualité
◷ 9am-10pm
Ⓢ 26/23FF

Piscine Suzanne Berlioux
A 50m swimming pool, surrounded by a tropical garden inside Paris' largest shopping mall. Busy, but fun never-the-less.
✉ Forum des Halles, 1er (5, B7) ☎ 01 42 36 98 44 Ⓜ Les Halles
◷ 10am-10pm
Ⓢ 25/20FF

out & about

WALKING TOURS
Serene Seine Stroll

The secret of this lovely walk is to savour the view from each bridge.

Cross Pont Marie **(1)** to charming Île St-Louis, browsing in the boutiques and taking the stairs to the eastern tip of the island.

Sample a *Berthillon* ice cream **(2)** as you cross Pont St-Louis to the Île de la Cité. Visit the Mémorial des Martyrs de la Déportation **(3)**, then wander through Square Jean XXIII **(4)** for a close encounter with Notre Dame **(5)**. Follow Quai aux Fleurs through the flower markets **(6)** to the Tour de l'Horloge and the Conciergerie **(7)**. Pass the Palais de Justice and Sainte Chapelle **(8)**, and take Quai des Orfèvres to secluded Place Dauphine **(9)**.

Carefully cross Pont Neuf to picnic in the Square du Vert Galant **(10)**, overlooked by the statue of Henri IV.

Wave to the passing boats from the Pont des Arts **(11)** before heading through the Cour Carrée of the Musée du Louvre **(12)** to the glass pyramid **(13)**. Pass under the Arc de Triomphe du Carrousel **(14)** to reach the Jardin des Tuileries **(15)**. Stroll through the gardens to emerge at Pont de la Concorde **(16)**. Pass Pont Alexandre III **(17)**, the Diana memorial **(18)** and the Jardins du Trocadéro **(19)**, and finish the walk with a fabulous view of the Tour Eiffel **(20)**.

Pont Neuf, Paris' oldest bridge

Simon Bracken

distance 7km **duration** 3hrs
start Ⓜ Pont Marie
end Ⓜ Trocadéro

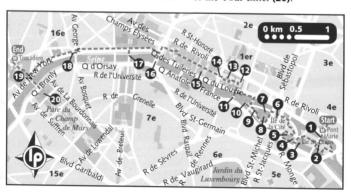

Marvellous Marais Ramble

From BHV department store **(1)**, saunter along cafe-lined rue des Archives. Turn right at the Archives Nationales **(2)**, left past the Hôtel de Rohan **(3)** and right again until Place de Thorigny. From here you can visit the Musée Picasso **(4)** or Musée de la Serrure-Bricard **(5)**, or continue to lovely little Square Léopold Achille **(6)** or Square Georges Cain **(7)** for a picnic.

Turn left into rue des Francs Bourgeois, passing the Musée Carnavalet **(8)**, to reach the impressive Place des Vosges **(9)**.

A door in the south-west corner leads through the courtyards of the Hôtel de Sully **(10)** to bustling rue St-Antoine. Turn right, and after a detour to Place du Marché Ste-Catherine **(11)**, right again into rue Pavée for the Guimard Synagogue **(12)**. Turn left into rue des Rosiers, the heart of the Jewish quarter, and grab a kosher felafel at *Chez Marianne* **(13)** if you're peckish.

A left into rue Vieille du Temple takes you across rue de Rivoli into St-Paul. Spicy rue François Miron, rue de Jouy and rue de l'Ave Maria lead to the Hôtel de Sens **(14)**. Learn a trick or two at the Musée de la Curiosité et de la Magie **(15)** in Village St-Paul, and follow ancient rue Charlemagne to glimpse a remnant of the 12th-century city wall **(16)**. The walk ends at the St-Paul metro via tiny rue du Prévôt.

SIGHTS & HIGHLIGHTS

Musée Picasso (p. 24)
Musée de la Serrure-Bricard (p. 35)
Musée Carnavalet (p. 33)
Place des Vosges (p. 20)
Hôtel de Sully (p. 37)
Guimard Synagogue (p. 40)

Rob Flynn

Hôtel de Sully

distance 3.5km **duration** 2½hrs
start Ⓜ Hôtel de Ville
end Ⓜ St-Paul

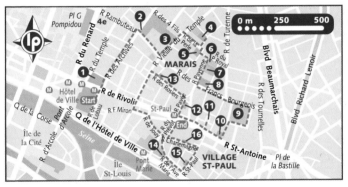

Left Bank Loop

From the Fontaine St-Michel **(1)** cross busy blvd St-Michel and meander through the warren of streets around rue de la Huchette **(2)** and Église St-Séverin **(3)**. Cross the road to Église St-Julien-le-Pauvre and Square Viviani **(4)**, then browse through the books at Shakespeare and Company **(5)**.

Follow the riverside *quais*, and turn right into rue des Fossés St-Bernard, passing the Institut du Monde Arabe **(6)**. A left into rue Jussieu then right into rue Linné brings you to the Roman Arènes de Lutèce **(7)**. Going down the hill, stroll through the Jardin des Plantes **(8)** or stop for mint tea at the Mosquée de Paris **(9)**.

Rue Daubenton takes you to funky rue Mouffetard **(10)**. Wind your way up the narrow market street, noting George Orwell's former down-and-out digs at 6 rue Pot-de-Fer **(11)**, and grab a bite to eat at *La Chope Café* in Place de la Contrescarpe **(12)**. Note the building Ernest Hemingway once called home at 74 rue du Cardinal Lemoine **(13)** and continue along rue Descartes, turning left into rue Clovis for Église St-Étienne du Mont **(14)** and the Panthéon **(15)**.

Follow busy rue Soufflot, with the Sorbonne **(16)** on your right, to the Jardin du Luxembourg **(17)**. Cobbled rue Servandoni **(18)** leads to massive Église St-Sulpice **(19)** and the chic shopping *quartier* to the north around Place du Quebec **(20)**. Cross blvd St-Germain to the Église St-Germain des Prés **(21)**, with the famous cafes *Deux Magots* and *Café de Flore* **(22)** to your left. Behind the church, visit pretty Place de Furstemberg **(23)** before taking bustling rue de Buci and rue St-André des Arts back to St-Michel.

distance 6km **duration** 3hrs
start Ⓜ St-Michel
end Ⓜ St-Michel

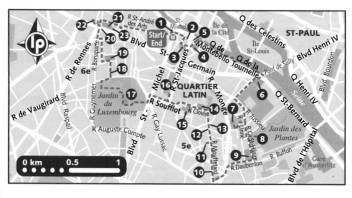

Montmartre Art Attack

Stride past saucy Moulin Rouge and Musée de l'Érotisme **(1)** up shop-lined rue Lepic. Detour left at rue des Abbesses to visit the Cimetière de Montmartre **(2)** and Van Gogh's home (3rd floor, No 54 rue Lepic) **(3)**.

Clamber up rue Tholozé **(4)** until you regain rue Lepic, with its 2 evocative windmills **(5 & 6)**. Turn left into rue Girardon, cross Square St-Buisson **(7)** and veer right through charming Allée des Brouillards (Fog Alley) **(8)**.

Descend the stairs from Place Dalida into rue St-Vincent, passing the Cimetière St-Vincent **(9)**. Turn right at the bohemian Lapin Agile **(10)** and stagger past the vineyard **(11)**. Turn left into rue Cortot, passing Montmartre's oldest house (now Musée de Montmartre) **(12)** and Eric Satie's house (No 6) **(13)**.

Turn right at the water tower **(14)** and left to reach Sacré Cœur

SIGHTS & HIGHLIGHTS

Cimetière de Montmartre (p. 21)
Basilique du Sacré Cœur (p. 21)
Espace Montmartre Salvador Dalí (p. 33)

Rob Flynn

Easel does it in Montmartre

(15) for a stunning vista over Paris. Walk past the funicular station and ancient St-Pierre de Montmartre **(16)** to touristy Place du Tertre **(17)**.

Follow rue Poulbot past the Dalí museum **(18)**. Descend the steps from Place du Calvaire **(19)** into rue Gabrielle, turning right to reach Place Émile Goudeau **(20)** and, at No 13, the rebuilt Bateau Lavoir studio where Picasso & Co set up their easels. Take the steps and turn left at rue des Abbesses to reach the Guimard-designed metro station at Place des Abbesses **(21)**.

distance 2.5km **duration** 2hrs
start Ⓜ Blanche
end Ⓜ Abbesses

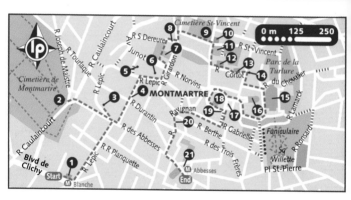

EXCURSIONS
Basilique de Saint Denis (1, B7)

Today Saint Denis is just another industrial suburb of Paris, but for 1200 years – from Dagobert I (629-39) to Louis XVIII (1814-24) – its basilica was the burial place of the kings of France, and a place of pilgrimage for living kings and popes. The ornate royal tombs, adorned with some truly remarkable statuary, and the basilica that contains them – the world's first major Gothic structure – are an easy half-day excursion by metro.

Nearby, the **Musée d'Art et d'Histoire** (☎ 01 42 43 05 10), 22bis rue Gabriel Péri, occupies a restored Carmelite convent founded in 1625 and later presided over by Louise de France, the youngest daughter of Louis XV. Displays include reconstructions of the Carmelites' cells, an 18th-century apothecary and, in the archaeology section, fascinating items found during excavations around Saint Denis (Wed-Mon 10am-5.30pm, Sun 2-6.30pm; 20/10FF).

INFORMATION

10km north of Paris
- Ⓜ Saint Denis-Basilique (line 13)
- 🚌 255, 256
- ☎ 01 48 09 83 54
- ⓘ tourist office (☎ 01 55 87 08 70), 1 rue de la République
- 🕐 10am-5pm (Sun from noon, Apr-Sept to 7pm)
- 💲 transept and chancel 32/21FF
- ♿ limited

Cathédrale de Chartres (1, E4)

The magnificent 13th-century Notre Dame de Chartres, dominating the **medieval town** and rich farmland from which it rises, is one of the crowning architectural achievements of western civilisation. The cathedral's astonishing original **stained-glass windows** (renowned for their intense blue tones), ornamented **portals** and 2 soaring spires – one Gothic, the other Romanesque – make it a must-do day trip from Paris.

The cathedral's collection of **relics** – particularly the Sainte Chemise, a piece of cloth said to have been worn by the Virgin Mary when she gave birth to Jesus – attracted many pilgrims during the Middle Ages.

The adjacent **Musée des Beaux-Arts** (☎ 02 37 36 41 39), 29 Cloître Notre Dame, includes mid-16th-century enamels of the 12 Apostles crafted by Léonard Limosin for François I, paintings from the 16th-19th centuries and wooden sculptures from the Middle Ages (Wed-Mon 10am-noon & 2-5pm, Apr-Oct to 6pm; 10/5FF).

INFORMATION

90km south of Paris
- 🚆 Gare Montparnasse to Chartres
- ☎ 02 37 21 56 33
- ⓘ tourist office (☎ 02 37 21 50 00), Place de la Cathédrale
- 🕐 7.30am-7.15pm (Sun from 8.30am)
- 💲 cathedral and treasury free; Clocher Neuf (New Bell Tower) 20FF (free under 12); English-language tours (☎ 02 37 28 15 58) Mon-Sat noon & 2.45pm 30FF; crypte tours 11/8FF
- ♿ limited

Château de Versailles   (1, C6)

The grandest and most famous château in France was the kingdom's political capital and the seat of the royal court between 1682 and 1789. Despite the crowds and queues, it makes a fascinating day trip from Paris – especially on a fine day when visitors can enjoy the immense gardens.

The enormous château was built in the mid-1600s during the reign of Louis XIV (the Sun King) as a symbol of the absolute power of the French monarchy, wreaking havoc on the kingdom's finances in the process. Some 30,000 workers and soldiers toiled to complete the structure.

The complex consists of 4 main parts: the palace building, the vast gardens west of the palace and 2 smaller palaces – the Grand Trianon and Petit Trianon. Palace highlights include the dazzling **Galeries des Glaces** (Hall of Mirrors; best in the late afternoon), **Opéra Royal**, the **Chapelle Royale** and the **Grands Appartements**.

INFORMATION

23km west of Paris

- 🚇 RER line C; SNCF from Gare St-Lazare or Gare Montparnasse
- ☎ 01 30 83 77 88
- 🄴 www.chateauversailles.fr
- ⓘ tourist office (☎ 01 39 50 36 22), 2bis ave de Paris, Versailles; tours in English
- ⊘ château Tues-Sun 9am-5.30pm (May-Sept to 6.30pm); gardens 7am-dusk (Oct-Apr from 8am)
- ⑤ château 45/35FF (free under 18); gardens free, except for concerts (Sun Apr-Oct; Sat Jul-Aug); Grand Trianon 25/15FF; Petit Trianon 15/10FF
- ⛬ limited
- ✕ cafe, La Flottille Restaurant

Let Them Eat Cake

On 5 October 1789, a mob of women protesting about bread shortages marched the 23km from Paris to Versailles. Marie-Antoinette escaped the mob using a secret passage, but the next day, after several of the demonstrators and palace guardsmen had been killed, both Louis XVI and his queen were dragged back to Paris – never to see Versailles again.

King Neptune and offspring, just one of Versailles' many statues

Diana Mayfield

Musée Claude Monet – Giverny   (1, A4)

The small village of Giverny was the home of impressionist Claude Monet from 1883-1926 and where he painted his famous *Décorations des Nymphéas* (Water Lilies). Each year more than 400,000 visitors make the pilgrimage to see his famous pastel pink-and-green house, Water Lily studio and flower-filled gardens.

The gardens change with the seasons. From early to late spring, daffodils, tulips, rhododendrons and irises appear, followed by poppies and lilies. By June, nasturtiums, roses and sweet pea are in flower. Around September, there are dahlias, sunflowers and hollyhocks. And, of course, the wisteria-clad Japanese bridge, the pond and water lilies.

Just down the road is the **Musée Américain** (☎ 02 32 51 94 65; 20/15FF) containing the works of many American impressionists who flocked to France early in the 20th century.

INFORMATION

76km west of Paris

🚉 Gare St-Lazare to Vernon, then bus

☎ 02 32 51 28 21

🕐 Apr-Oct Tues-Sun 10am-6pm

💲 35/25/20FF

♿ limited

Spring tulips at Giverny

Monet's house, Giverny

ORGANISED TOURS

You'll find a wide variety of tours (mostly in French) advertised in *L'Officiel des Spectacles* and *Pariscope*, under the headings *promenades* or *conférences*.

BICYCLE TOURS

Paris à Vélo c'est Sympa (3, G15)
Michel Nöe offers a range of interesting (even quirky) half-day thematic bike tours (English spoken), covering central and outer Paris; also dawn, night and full-day (summer) excursions.

✉ 37 blvd Bourdon, 4e
☎ 01 48 87 60 01
🄮 www.parisvelosympa.com ⑤ 170/150FF half-day; 190/170FF at night

Paris Vélo (3, K13)
Well-organised bilingual tours of major sightseeing areas such as the Marais, Île St-Louis and Quartier Latin, plus an ad-libbed night tour.

✉ 2 rue du Fer à Moulin, 5e ☎ 01 43 37 59 22 ⑤ 150-180FF half-day

BOAT TOURS

Bateaux Mouches
(3, D4) Bateaux Mouches runs the biggest tour boats on the Seine. Cruises depart/return Pont de l'Alma, and pass the Statue of Liberty and Tour Eiffel in the west, and Île St-Louis in the east; cruises last 1¼hrs.

✉ Pont de l'Alma, 8e
☎ 01 42 25 96 10; English-language recording ☎ 01 40 76 99 99 🄮 www.bateauxmouches.com ◷ summer every 30mins 10am-8pm, every 20mins 8-11pm; winter 11am, 2.30, 4, 6 & 9pm ⑤ 40/20FF; 330/150FF

lunch; 500-700FF dinner (smart dress)

Bateaux Parisiens
(3, E2) One-hour Seine cruises with commentary in multiple languages. The 2hr lunch/3hr dinner cruises include meals and wine.

✉ Port de la Bourdonnais, 7e
☎ 01 44 11 33 55
🄮 www.bateauxparisiens.com ◷ Easter-Oct every 30mins 10am-10.30pm; Nov-Easter every hr 10am-9pm ⑤ 50/25FF; 300FF lunch; 560-750FF dinner

Canauxrama (3, G15)
Three-hour cruises along charming Canal St-Martin and Canal de l'Ourcq between Port de l'Arsenal and Parc de la Villette.

Bicycle tour through the streets of the Marais

DIY River Tour

From April to October the **Batobus** river shuttle (☎ 01 44 11 33 99) runs every 25mins between 10am and 7pm (Jul-Aug to 9pm). Tickets start at 20/10FF or 60/30FF for a day pass. Jump aboard at:

- Tour Eiffel
- Musée d'Orsay
- St-Germain des Prés
- Notre Dame
- Hôtel de Ville
- Musée du Louvre

✉ Port de l'Arsenal, opp 50 blvd de la Bastille, 12e; Bassin de la Villette, 13 Quai de la Loire, 19e (2, B12) ☎ 01 42 39 15 00 ⏲ From Parc de la Villette 9.45am & 2.45pm; from Port de l'Arsenal 9.45am & 2.30pm ⑤ 75/60/45FF; Sat & Sun 75FF

Cruising along the Seine

Richard I'Anson

Paris Canal Croisières

Three-hour cruise along the Seine and canals from the Musée d'Orsay to Parc de la Villette.

✉ Quai Anatole France (3, E7) or Parc de la Villette (2, B13) ☎ 01 42 40 96 97 ⏲ late Mar-mid-Nov depart Musée d'Orsay 9.30am, return Parc de la Villette 2.30pm; mid-July-Aug also from

museum 2.35pm & park 6.15pm ⑤ 100/75/60FF

Vedettes du Pont Neuf (5, A5)

This company offers 1hr boat excursions and lunch and dinner cruises.

✉ sq du Vert Galant, Île de la Cité, 1er ☎ 01 46 33 98 38 ⏲ summer every 30mins 10am-noon, 1.30-6.30pm & 9-10.30pm; winter 3 per day Mon-Thurs, 7 per day Fri-Sun ⑤ 50/25FF; lunch 290/150FF; dinner 350/470FF

BUS TOURS

Balabus

'See Paris through the window of a bus' every Sunday afternoon from April-Sept. RATP's Balabus follows a 1hr route from Gare de Lyon to La Défense, passing many of central Paris' most famous sights. Details available at metro counters.

Paris l'Open Tour – get on, get off ...

✉ Gare de Lyon (2, G12) or La Défense Grande Arche (2, B1) ⏲ Every 15-30mins 1.30-8.30pm (Gare de Lyon) & 12.30-8pm (La Défense) ☎ 08 36 68 41 14 ⑤ 135/70FF

Cityrama (3, D9)

Cityrama runs 2hr tours of the city (multi-language taped commentary) and night city tours in high-tech buses with panoramic windows, and also offers a range of excursions further afield.
✉ 147 rue St-Honoré, 1er ☎ 01 44 55 61 00 ✆ www.cityrama.com ⑤ 150FF; Chartres 270FF; Versailles 195FF

Paris l'Open Tour

London-style double-decker buses travel a 2¼hr circuit that takes in Notre Dame, the Tour Eiffel and Musée d'Orsay as well as the usual list of Right Bank tourist sights. Over 2 consecutive days you can get on and off these buses wherever you like; commentary in English and French.
✉ tour begins and ends at Place de la Madeleine, 8e (3, B7) ⏲ 9.45am-6.05pm ☎ 01 53 95 39 53 ⑤ 135/70FF

RICKSHAW TOURS
Vélo Taxi

Bilingual students pedal bright yellow cycle-rickshaws for a 1hr tour of the sights around Place de la Concorde. Departing from the Tuileries gate, the tours pass La Madeleine, Opéra, Place Vendôme, the Musée d'Orsay and the Louvre.
✉ 12 rue Vignon, 9e (3, B8) ☎ 01 47 42 00 01 ⏲ Apr-Oct 10am-

DIY Bus Tours

With a little ingenuity, and for the cost of a metro ticket, you can devise your own tour on an RATP bus. Bus No 29 has an open-air platform at the back.

Bus Nos 21 or 27
Opéra, Palais Royal, Louvre, Pont Neuf, Jardin du Luxembourg, Panthéon
Bus No 29
Opéra, Centre Pompidou, Marais, Place des Vosges, Bastille, Gare de Lyon
Bus No 47
Centre Pompidou, Notre Dame, Arènes de Lutèce, Gobelins
Bus No 63
Musée d'Orsay, Trocadéro, Concorde, Invalides
Bus No 73
Concorde, Champs Élysées, Arc de Triomphe
Bus No 82
Montparnasse, Invalides, Tour Eiffel

6pm ⑤ 90/130FF (1/2 passengers)

VIDEO TOUR
Paristoric

Audiovisual hourly excursion through Paris' 2000-year history. Designed mainly for school-age children, but even the oldies may learn a thing or two. Headset commentary in choice of languages.
✉ 11bis rue Scribe, 9e (3, B8) ☎ 01 42 66 62 06 ✆ www.paristoric.com ⏲ Apr-Oct 9am-8pm; Nov-Mar 9am-6pm ⑤ 50/40/30FF

WALKING TOURS
Bohemian Paris

Tours of the bohemian Left Bank led by American expat writer and scholar Gentry Lane. Visit the haunts of Jazz Age artists from James Joyce to Josephine Baker.
✉ 8 rue Bréa, 6e (3, J8) ☎ 01 56 24 36 00 ⑤ 200FF

Paris Walking Tours

Peter and Oriel Caine and their small English-speaking team offer 2hr daily walks through Paris, including Montmartre, the Marais and the Paris of Hemingway and Jefferson.
✉ 12 Passage Meunier, 93200 Saint Denis (1, C7) ☎ 01 48 09 21 40 ✆ www.pariswalking tours.com ⑤ 60/40/30FF

Promenade Litteraire

The Bibliothèque Publique d'Information (BPI), part of the Centre Pompidou, organises excellent literary tours that follow in the footsteps of such diverse writers as Céline, Rilke, Georges Simenon, Jean Cocteau and Henry Miller.
✉ 11 rue Brantôme, 3e (3, E12) ☎ 01 44 78 45 73 ⏲ Wed 2.30pm, Sun 10am & 2.30pm ⑤ 100/80FF

shopping

Détaxe

If you're not a resident of the EU, you can get a TVA (sales tax) refund of up to 17.1%, provided you have spent more than 1200FF in any one store. You fill out a form in the store (you'll need your passport number), and then take the form and purchased goods to the customs desk at the point you leave the EU (allow at least 3hrs before flights). The refund is usually credited to your credit-card account or mailed by cheque within 3 months of your leaving the EU.

Hot Shop Spots

Paris' main shopping areas are:

Abbesses, 18e – vintage clothing, streetwear, fabrics, music

Marais, 3e – hip boutiques, books & music, homewares and quirky speciality stores

Opéra, 9e – major department stores, clothing, perfume, cosmetics

Place Vendôme, 1er – jewellery, luxury goods

Quartier Latin, 5e – bookshops, stationery

rue de Paradis, 10e – glass, crystal, china, Limoges ware

rue de Rivoli & Les Halles, 1er & 2e – international brands, clothes, shoes, books & music, toys, perfume

St-Germain, 6e – designer clothes and accessories, antiques, speciality stores

St-Paul, 4e – antiques, paper goods & stationery

Sentier, 2e – wholesale garments, fabrics and jewellery

Triangle d'Or & rue du Faubourg St-Honoré, 8e & 1er – haute couture, jewellery & luxury goods, art galleries

Viaduc des Arts, 12e – boutiques, designers and galleries

Paris is a sublime place to shop, whether you're someone who can afford an original Cartier diamond bracelet or you're an impecunious *lèche-vitrine* ('window licker'). From the ultra-chic couture houses to the boutiques of the Marais, Paris is a city that knows how to make it, how to present it – and how to charge for it.

Unlike many cities, Paris doesn't really have a shopping downtown: browsing is a fascinating way to discover hidden parts of the city. Many *quartiers* still specialise in a single product or art, and the myriad boutiques – still the heart and soul of Paris shopping – are often worth a visit in themselves.

Credit cards are accepted everywhere (Visa is the most common), but not travellers cheques. Many stores, in particular large department stores and 'duty-free' stores, will give foreign-passport holders discounts of 10% or more if you ask; but bargaining is frowned upon, except at flea markets.

Opening Hours

Opening hours in Paris are notoriously anarchic, with each store setting its own hours according to some ancient black art. Most stores open at least 10am-6pm, 5 days a week, including Saturday; but they may open earlier, close later, close for lunch (usually 1-2.30pm) or for a full or half-day on Monday or Tuesday. Many larger stores also have a *nocturne* – 1 late night a week (up to 10pm). Many smaller stores close completely in August. Only shops in some tourist areas (eg the Champs Élysées and the Marais) open on Sunday.

DEPARTMENT STORES

Au Bon Marché
(3, G7) Paris' first department store, built by Gustave Eiffel, is less frenetic than its rivals across the river, but no less chic. Men's as well as women's fashions are well represented. The glorious grocery store, La Grande Épicerie de Paris, is in store No 2, with all your picnic needs.

✉ 24 rue de Sèvres, 7e
☎ 01 44 39 80 00
Ⓜ Sèvres Babylone
⊘ Mon-Sat 9.30am-7pm; grocery store 8.30am-9pm

BHV (Bazar de l'Hôtel de Ville)
(5, C7) BHV is a straightforward department store – apart from its enormous and chaotic hardware/DIY department in the *sous sol* (basement), with every type of hammer, power tool, nail, plug or hinge you could ask for (which is what you'll have to do, since you'll never find it on your own).

✉ 52-64 rue de Rivoli, 4e ☎ 01 42 74 90 00
Ⓜ Hôtel de Ville
⊘ Mon-Sat 9.30am-7pm (Wed to 10pm)

Galeries Lafayette
(3, B9) This vast store, with over 75,000 brand-name items, has everything under 2 roofs: fashion (Vivienne Westwood to Gap), shoes and accessories, perfume and cosmetics, lingerie, men's clothing, homewares, books and music – the lot. There's a fantastic view from the rooftop restaurants.

✉ 40 blvd Haussmann, 9e ☎ 01 42 82 34 56
Ⓜ Auber; Chaussée d'Antin ⊘ Mon-Sat 9.30am-7pm (Thurs to 9pm)

Marks & Spencer
(3, B8) Just the ticket if you can't survive Paris without your M&S knickers, cashmere jumper or faux crabmeat on whiter-than-white bread.

✉ 35 blvd Haussmann, 9e and 88 rue de Rivoli, 4e (3, F12) 9e: ☎ 01 47 42 42 91; 4e: ☎ 01 45 38 52 87 Ⓜ 9e: Auber or Chaussée d'Antin; 4e: Hôtel de Ville ⊘ Mon-Sat 9am-8pm (Tues from 9.30am, Thurs to 9pm)

Le Printemps
(3, B8) Actually 3 separate stores – 1 each for women's and men's fashion and 1 for the home – Printemps offers a staggering display of perfume, cosmetics and accessories, as well as established and up-and-coming designer wear. There's a fashion show every Tuesday (and Friday March to October) at 10am on the 7th floor under the cupola.

✉ 64 blvd Haussmann, 9e ☎ 01 42 82 50 00
Ⓜ Havre Caumartin
⊘ Mon-Sat 9.35am-7pm (Thurs to 10pm)

La Samaritaine
(5, A6) It may not have the status of Galeries Lafayette or Printemps, but Samaritaine offers an excellent range of goods across its 4 stores. There's a stunning (and free) view of Paris from the rooftop terrace of store 2, while newly renovated store 4 is dedicated to men.

✉ 19 rue de la Monnaie, 1er ☎ 01 40 41 20 20 Ⓜ Pont Neuf
⊘ Mon-Sat 9.30am-7pm (Thurs to 10pm)

Tati (4, D9)
With its warcry of *les plus bas prix* (lowest prices) – and quality to match – Tati has been Paris' great working-class department store for 50 years. Don't be surprised to see trendy Parisians searching for street cred and fighting for bargains hidden in the oddments bins and piled onto tables.

✉ 4 blvd Barbès, 18e; branches at 140 rue de Rennes, 6e, and 13 Place de la République, 3e ☎ 01 55 29 50 00
Ⓜ Barbès Rochechouart
⊘ Mon 10am-7pm, Tues-Fri 9.30am-7pm, Sat 9.15am-7pm

Glorious Galeries Lafayette

CLOTHING & ACCESSORIES

All of the Parisian couturiers have their own boutiques in the capital (some, like YSL, have several), but it's also possible to see impressive designer collections at major department stores such as Le Printemps, Galeries Lafayette and Au Bon Marché. The Right Bank is traditionally the epicentre of Parisian fashion.

The ultra-exclusive **Triangle d'Or** (Golden Triangle) between Place de l'Alma and the Champs Élysées and the long, narrow rue du Faubourg St-Honoré/rue St-Honoré are the home of *haute couture*. Here are the opulent boutiques of Prada, Inès de la Fressange, Celine, Chanel, Valentino, Nina Ricci, Thierry Mugler, Givenchy, Hermès, Guy Laroche and Christian Lacroix.

Just to the east, around **Place des Victoires** and **Église St-Eustache**, designers include Kenzo, Cacharel, Stephane Kélian, Thierry Mugler, Comme des Garçons, Yohji Yamamoto, Chevignon Trading Post, Junko Shimada, Jean-Paul Gaultier and agnès b.

Further east again, the narrow rue des Rosiers and rue des Francs Bourgeois in the **Marais** attract a growing number of hip designer outlets – Tehen, L'Éclaireur, Lolita Lempicka, Martin Grant – plus some accessory shops.

Many of the big names have jumped the river to the chic shopping district of the **6e**, north and west of Place St-Sulpice: Il Bisonte, Sonia Rykiel, Celine, Kenzo, Benetton, Yves Saint Laurent Rive Gauche and Boutique Femme are all here.

If you're looking for expensive baubles, double-park the limo at **Place Vendôme** for a quick whip around Cartier, Philippe Patek, Van Cleef & Arpels and Bucheron. Funkier items, many of them imported, can be found in the **Marais** or along the **Viaduc des Arts**, while costume jewellery can be found at the flea markets or in the Temple area near République.

Lacroix

Dior

Lacroix

écile et Jeanne

écile and Jeanne are 2 oung jewellery designers making a splash in Paris with their colourful and rty jewellery and accessories. They have several ocations in the city.

☒ 215 rue St-Honoré, er (3, D8); 12 rue des rancs Bourgeois, 3e (3, 14); 49 ave Daumesnil Viaduc des Arts), 12e 2, G12) ☎ 01 42 61 8 68 (1er) Ⓜ Tuileries; t-Paul; Bastille ◷ Mon-Sat 11am-7pm

Colette

robably the most talked bout store in Paris in the ast few years, Japanese-nspired Colette is an ode to tyle over all else. Its selec-ion and display of clothes, accessories and odds & nds is exquisite. Featured esigners include Alexander McQueen, Alberta Ferretti nd Lulu Guinness.

☒ 213 rue St-Honoré, er (3, D8) ☎ 01 55 35 3 90 Ⓜ Tuileries ◷ 10.30am-7.30pm

Didier Ludot

A fabulous store crammed vith pre-loved couture reations from yesteryear,

Lacroix

Couturier Addresses

agnès b 6 rue du Jour, 1er (3, D11)
Calvin Klein 45 ave Montaigne, 8e (3, C4)
Christian Dior 30 ave Montaigne, 8e (3, C4)
Dolce e Gabbana 2 ave Montaigne, 8e (3, C4)
Emporio Armani 149 blvd St-Germain, 6e (5, A3)
Hermès 24 rue du Faubourg St-Honoré, 8e (3, C6)
Issey Miyake 3 Place des Vosges, 4e (5, E8)
Jean-Paul Gaultier 30 rue du Faubourg St-Antoine, 12e (2, F12)
Kenzo 3 Place des Victoires, 1er (3, D10)
Paco Rabanne 7 rue du Cherche-Midi, 6e (3, G8)
Prada 10 ave Montaigne, 8e (3, C4)
Sonia Rykiel 175 blvd St-Germain, 6e (3, F8)
Yohji Yamamoto 3 rue de Grenelle, 6e (3, G8)
Yves Saint Laurent 6 Place St-Sulpice, 6e (5, A2)

including original Chanel suits from the 1950s and Hermès bags and accessories – all sold for half the original price.

☒ 20-24 Galerie de Montpensier, 1er (3, D9) ☎ 01 42 96 06 56 Ⓜ Palais Royal ◷ Mon-Sat 10.30am-7pm

Divine

An extraordinarily comprehensive range of new and pre-doffed headwear for both men and women, from straw boaters to Basque berets and velvet cloches.

☒ 39 rue Daguerre, 14 (2, H8) ☎ 01 43 22 28 10 Ⓜ Denfert Rochereau ◷ Tues-Sat 10.30am-1pm & 3-7.30pm

L'Épicerie

Part art space, part lounge, part deconstructionist fashion statement, this funky little boutique tucked away in a Marais courtyard features the work of several young designers, as well as its own lines and some handsome limited-edition jewellery.

☒ 30 rue du Temple, 3e (5, C7) ☎ 01 42 78

12 39 Ⓜ Hôtel de Ville ◷ Tues-Sat 11am-9pm

Kiliwatch

Enormous barn filled with rack after rack of colourfully original street and club-wear, plus a startling range of quality second-hand clothes and accessories.

☒ 64 rue Tiquetonne, 21 (3, D11) ☎ 01 42 21 17 37 Ⓜ Étienne Marcel ◷ Mon 1-7pm, Tues-Sat 10.30am-9pm

Madelios

The recently renovated Madelios is a one-stop shop for men, including a fine selection of classic and modern suits, shoes and casual wear, a hairdressing salon, cafe and exhibition space.

☒ 23 blvd de la Madeleine, 8e (3, C8) ☎ 01 42 60 39 30 Ⓜ Madeleine ◷ 10.30am-7pm

Le Mouton à Cinq Pattes

The 'sheep with 5 legs' specialises in heavily discounted designer clothing from last year's range. All items are new but most are *dégriffé* (their labels have been torn out). If you know your Jean-Paul Gaultier from your Vivienne Westwood, you can walk away with a 70% discount.

✉ **19 rue Grégoire de Tours, 6e (5, B3); 15 rue du Vieille du Temple, 4e (5, D7)**
☎ **01 43 29 73 56 (6e)**
Ⓜ **Sévres Babylone; Hôtel de Ville** ☺ **Mon-Sat 10.30am-7.30pm, Sat 10.30am-8pm**

Réciproque
Réciproque has a huge range of high-quality second-hand couture and designer clothing, shoes and accessories for both women and men, at around half the original price.

✉ **95 rue de la Pompe, 16e (2, E4)**
☎ **01 47 04 30 28**
Ⓜ **Rue de la Pompe** ☺ **Tues-Fri 11am-7.30pm, Sat 10.30am-7.30pm**

Spleen
Stunning showcase for a range of new *créateurs*, many from Italy and the UK, among them John Richmond, Lawrence Steel, Emilio Cavallini and Joerg Hartmann. There's also a hanging space for original fashion photography.

✉ **3bis rue des Rosiers, 4e (5, D7)**
☎ **01 42 74 65 66**
Ⓜ **St-Paul** ☺ **Mon 3-7pm, Tues-Sat 11am-7pm, Sun 2-7pm**

PERFUME & COSMETICS

Paris is still one of the best places to buy perfume and cosmetics. Not only is the range enormous (with many fragrances, colours and products that never reach overseas markets), but prices are often lower and the quality better. Plus you can often find that special product that's been discontinued at home. The big department stores (see p. 59) have wide selections, or head for the specialist shops.

Guerlain
Guerlain is Paris' most famous perfumerie, and its shop, dating from 1912, is one of the most beautiful in the city; with its shimmering mirror and marble decor, it's a reminder of the former glory of the Champs Élysées. Many Guerlain fragrances are available only through Guerlain boutiques.

✉ **68 ave des Champs Élysées, 8e (3, B4)**
☎ **01 45 62 52 57**
Ⓜ **Franklin D Roosevelt** ☺ **Mon-Sat 9.45am-7pm, Sun 3-7pm**

Séphora
Séphora's flagship megastore features over 12,000 fragrances and cosmetics, most of which are available for sampling with no pressure to buy.

✉ **70 ave des Champs Élysées, 8e (3, B4)**

☎ **01 53 93 22 50**
Ⓜ **Franklin D Roosevelt** ☺ **Mon-Sat 10am-midnight, Sun noon-midnight**

Shiseido
This exquisite salon in the arcades of the Palais Royal is the showcase for

Chanel No 5

Simon Bracken

the olfactory genius of Serge Lutens, and well worth a visit just for a sniff – or for a custom-designed scent.

✉ **142 Galerie de Valois, 1er (3, D10)**
☎ **01 49 27 09 09**
Ⓜ **Louvre; Palais Royal** ☺ **Mon-Sat 9am-7pm**

Shu Uemura
Colour your world with the palettes of this cult Japanese make-up magician – over 100 shades of lippie, blusher and eyeshadow. Have half your face made up by the knowledgeable beauticians, and do the other half yourself under their watchful eye.

✉ **176 blvd St-Germain, 6e (5, A3)**
☎ **01 45 48 02 55**
Ⓜ **St-Germain des Prés** ☺ **Mon 11am-7pm, Tues-Sat 10am-7pm**

ART & ANTIQUES

Paris' high-quality antique dealers congregate in the rue du Faubourg St-Honoré and the Carré Rive Gauche (just to the east of the Musée d'Orsay). There are also a number of shops selling antique furniture, maps and antiquarian books around rue Bonaparte and rue Jacob in the 6e and the Village St-Paul, 4e.

Art galleries cluster around ave Matignon (8e), Beaubourg (3e), St-Germain (6e) and Bastille (11e/12e). Recently, several new galleries in rue Louise Weiss (13e), behind the new Bibliothèque Nationale, have created a buzz with their avant-garde conceptual works. Exhibitions are listed in *Pariscope* and *L'Officiel des Spectacles*, or check out www.vianet.fr for details. Many galleries close in August.

Drouot-Richelieu

Paris' best known auction house has been selling fine lots for nearly 150 years. Bidding is in (fast) French and a 10-15% house commission is charged on top of the purchase price. Payment in cash or by French cheque. Auction details are in the *Gazette de l'Hôtel Drouot* at newsstands.

✉ 9 rue Drouot, 9e (3, B10) ☎ 01 48 00 20 20 📧 www.gazette-drouot.com Ⓜ Richelieu Drouot ⏲ sales 2-6pm; viewing 11am-6pm day prior and 11am-noon sale day

Galerie Adrian Maeght

One of the best known galleries in Paris – where the work of Braque, Giacometti, Del Rey and Miró once hung – still displays an impressive array of modern works; there's also a fine art bookstore, with many volumes produced in-house.

✉ 42 rue du Bac, 7e (3, F8) ☎ 01 45 48 45 15 Ⓜ Rue du Bac ⏲ Tues-Sat 9.30am-7pm

Galerie Durand-Dessert (2, F12)

Probably the strongest of the new-wave Bastille-quartier galleries, featuring the work of artists Yan Pei Ming and Gérard Garouste, and photographers William Wegman, Patrick Tosani and Balthasar Burkhard.

✉ 28 rue de Lappe, 11e ☎ 01 48 06 92 23 Ⓜ Bastille ⏲ Tues-Sat 11am-7pm

Galerie Jennifer Flay

(2, H12) What's a Kiwi doing flogging conceptual art in Paris? A very fine job, according to the cognoscenti. Jennifer Flay offers a good intro to (and explanation of) the *ScèneEst* scene.

✉ 20 rue Louise Weiss, 13e ☎ 01 44 06 73 60 Ⓜ Chevaleret ⏲ Tues-Fri 2-7pm, Sat 11am-7pm

Le Louvre des Antiquaires (3, E10)

Some 250 elegant antique shops cluster on 3 floors of this impressive building on the eastern side of Place du Palais Royal. Each is filled with original (and expensive) furniture, clocks, *objets d'art*, classical antiquities and (in the basement) jewellery.

✉ 2 Place du Palais Royal, 1er ☎ 01 42 97 27 00 Ⓜ Palais Royal ⏲ Tues-Sun 11am-7pm

Time Passages

Paris' *passages* or *galeries* are 19th-century shopping arcades, many sublimely preserved and well worth a detour.

Galerie Véro Dodat (3, D10; 19 rue Jean-Jacques Rousseau to 2 rue du Bouloi, 1er) opened in 1826 and specialises in antiques, objets d'art, and fashion accessories. In the **Passage du Grand Cerf** (3, D12; 145 rue St-Denis to 10 rue Dussoubs, 2e) you'll find modern jewellery and lighting designers; while the gorgeous **Galerie Vivienne** (3, D10; 6 rue Vivienne to 4 rue des Petits-Champs, 2e) has a fashion bent.

MUSIC & BOOKS

Paris is justly famous for the writers who have graced its cafes and boulevards. But a city's literary culture is only as good as its bookshops, and Paris has many excellent English-language ones. A vast selection of recorded music is available at the Virgin Megastore (3, C4) and FNAC (5, A7).

Abbey Bookshop
A mellow place, not far from Place St-Michel, known for having free tea and coffee, a supply of Canadian newspapers and a good selection of new and used works of fiction – plus readings of prose and poetry once a week, usually on Wednesday night.
✉ **29 rue de la Parcheminerie, 5e (5, C4)** ☎ **01 46 33 16 24** Ⓜ **Cluny La Sorbonne** 🕐 **Mon-Sat 10am-7pm**

Album
This shop specialises in adult *bandes dessinées* (comic books), which have an enormous following in France. Album has everything from *Tintin* to erotic and rare comics and French editions of the latest Japanese *manga*.
✉ **8 rue Dante, 5e (5, C4)** ☎ **01 43 25 85 19** Ⓜ **Maubert Mutualité**

Browsing at Shakespeare and Company

🕐 **Tues-Sat 10am-8pm**

Brentano's
Midway between the Louvre and Opéra Garnier, this is a good spot for tracking down books from the USA, including fiction, business titles and magazines, as well as a good range of kids' books.
✉ **37 ave de l'Opéra, 2e (3, C9)** ☎ **01 42 61 52 50** Ⓜ **Opéra** 🕐 **Mon-Sat 10am-7.30pm**

Institut Géographique National
A cartographer's delight – atlases, globes, walking maps, wine district maps, compasses, satellite images, historic maps and guidebooks to France and the rest of the world.
✉ **107 rue La Boétie, 8e (3, B4)** ☎ **01 43 98 85 00** ⊕ **www.ign.fr** Ⓜ **Franklin D Roosevelt** 🕐 **Mon-Fri 9.30am-7pm, Sat 11am-12.30pm & 2-6.30pm**

Librarie Gourmande
Not only do the French love to talk about food, they love to write about it as well, and Geneviève Baudon's tasteful bookshop is *the* place to discover the secrets of French food, wine and the culinary arts.
✉ **4 rue Dante, 5e (5, C4)** ☎ **01 43 54 37 27** Ⓜ **Maubert Mutualité** 🕐 **10am-7pm**

Les Mots à la Bouche
Paris' premier gay bookshop specialises in books written by homosexuals or with gay or lesbian themes, and periodicals, including some in English. Most of the back wall is dedicated to English-language books, including lots of novels. Videos and CDs are also on sale.
✉ **6 rue Ste-Croix de la Bretonnerie, 4e (5, C7)** ☎ **01 42 78 88 30** Ⓜ **Hôtel de Ville** 🕐 **Mon-Thurs 11am-11pm, Sun 2-8pm**

Shakespeare and Company
Paris' most famous English-language bookshop has a varied and unpredictable collection of new and used books in English and other languages. Poetry readings are held on most Mondays at 8pm. The shop is named after Sylvia Beach's bookshop – famous for publishing James Joyce's *Ulysses* in 1922 – which was closed by the Nazis in 1941.
✉ **37 rue de la Bûcherie, 5e (5, C5)** ☎ **01 43 26 96 50** Ⓜ **St-Michel** 🕐 **noon-midnight**

Village Voice
A friendly, helpful shop with an excellent selection of contemporary North American fiction and European literature in translation. It often sponsors readings, usually on Thursday at around 7pm.

✉ 6 rue Princesse, 6e (5, A3) ☎ 01 46 33 36 47 Ⓜ Mabillon ◷ Mon 2-8pm, Tues-Sat 10am-8pm

WH Smith
This branch of the English chain is situated 1 block east of Place de la Concorde, and offers a large selection of English-language titles and magazines. Brace yourself for the imported prices.
✉ 248 rue de Rivoli, 1er (3, D7) ☎ 01 44 77 88 99 Ⓜ Concorde ◷ Mon-Sat 9.30am-7pm, Sun 1-7pm

Ulysse
For 20 years Catherine Demain has been fuelling the wanderlust of Parisian travellers in this delightful store full of travel guides, maps, back issues of *National Geographic* and sage advice.
✉ 26 rue St-Louis en l'Île, 4e (5, E6) ☎ 01 43 25 17 35 🖂 www.ulysse.fr Ⓜ Pont Marie ◷ Tues-Sat 2-8pm

HOMEWARES & DESIGN

Axis
Everyday items (plates, vases, lights, juicers) with a wonderfully whimsical designer twist – most in snazzy colours and materials. A great place to find that *quelque chose de spéciale.*
✉ Marché St-Germain, 14 rue Lobineau, 6e (5, A3) & 13 rue de Charonne, 11e (2, F12) ☎ 01 43 29 66 23 Ⓜ Mabillon; Ledru Rollin ◷ Mon-Sat 10am-8pm

Bains Plus
Bathroom suppliers to the new millennium, including luxurious robes and gowns, soaps and oils, shaving brushes, mirrors ...
✉ 51 rue des Francs Bourgeois, 3e (5, C8) ☎ 01 48 87 83 07 Ⓜ Hôtel de Ville ◷ Tues-Sat 11am-7pm, Sun 2.30-7pm

E Dehillerin
This shop (founded in 1820) carries the most incredible selection of professional-quality cookware – you're sure to find something even the very best equipped kitchen is lacking.
✉ 18-20 rue Coquillière, 1er (3, D11) ☎ 01 42 36 53 13 Ⓜ Les Halles ◷ Mon-Sat 8am-6pm (closed Mon 12.30-2pm)

Les Milles Feuilles
Wonderfully disorganised little shop full of romantic gift ideas (for yourself, of course): flowers, candles, baskets, vases, what-nots and thingummy-jigs.
✉ 2 rue Rambuteau, 3e (5, C8) ☎ 01 42 78 32 93 Ⓜ Rambuteau ◷ 10am-8pm (Mon from 11am)

Bits & bobs & thingummy-jigs

FOOD & DRINK

You don't need to eat at restaurants to enjoy the best of French food. The *boulangeries*, *pâtisseries* and *traiteurs* throughout the city have an incredible selection of mouthwatering delights, whatever your mood or budget. Food can also make a great gift for envious friends at home.

À l'Olivier
The place in Paris for oil – from olive to walnut – with a good selection of vinegars, olives and mustards as well.
✉ 23 rue de Rivoli, 4e (5, D7) ☎ 01 48 04 86 59 Ⓜ St-Paul ⏱ Tues-Sat 9.30am-1pm & 2-7pm

Les Caves Augé
If Marcel Proust was any judge of wine shops, then go no further than Paris' oldest – now under the stewardship of passionate and knowledgeable *sommelier* Marc Sibard.
✉ 116 blvd Haussmann, 8e (3, A6) ☎ 01 45 22 16 97 Ⓜ St-Augustin ⏱ Mon-Sat 9am-7.30pm (Mon from 11am)

Boulangerie in the Jewish quarter

Hédiard window display

Fauchon
The most famous food store in Paris: 6 departments sell the most incredibly mouthwatering (and expensive) delicacies, from *foie gras* to *confitures*. The fruits – the most perfect you've ever seen – include exotic items from South-East Asia (mangosteens, rambutans etc). Fauchon also has several eat-in options.
✉ 26-30 Place de la Madeleine, 8e (3, B8) ☎ 01 47 62 60 11 Ⓜ Madeleine ⏱ Mon-Sat 9.40am-7pm

La Grande Épicerie de Paris
Get all your picnic supplies at this wonderful Left Bank gourmet delicatessen and supermarket.
✉ Store 2 Au Bon Marché, 38 rue de Sèvres, 7e (3, H7)

☎ 01 44 39 81 00 Ⓜ Sèvres Babylone ⏱ Mon-Sat 8.30am-9pm

Hédiard
This famous luxury food shop consists of 2 adjacent sections selling prepared dishes, tea, coffee, jams, wine, pastries, fruit and vegetables etc.
✉ 21 Place de la Madeleine, 8e (3, B7) ☎ 01 43 12 88 88 Ⓜ Madeleine ⏱ Mon-Sat 8am-10pm

Maison de la Truffe
If you've always wanted to snuffle fine truffles – French black from late October to March, Italian white mid-October to December (over 2000FF per 100g) – here's your chance. There's also a small sit-down area (open from noon to closing) where you can sample dishes made with the prized fungus.
✉ 19-21 Place de la Madeleine, 8e (3, B7) ☎ 01 45 65 53 22 Ⓜ Madeleine ⏱ Mon-Sat 9am-9pm (Mon to 8pm)

Mariage Frères
Paris' premier tea shop (founded in 1854) has around 500 varieties from 32 countries; the most expensive is a variety of Japanese *thé vert* (green tea) which costs about 50FF for 100g. In summer you can cool off in the 19th-century *salon de thé*

(tearoom) with a choice of 5 kinds of tea-flavoured ice cream. There are branches at 13 rue des Grands Augustins (6e) and 260 rue du Faubourg-St-Honoré (8e).

✉ **30-32 rue du Bourg Tibourg, 4e (5, C7)**
☎ 01 42 72 28 11
Ⓜ Hôtel de Ville
🕓 10.30am-7.30pm; tearoom 12-7pm

Richard Nebesky

Pretty as a pâtisserie

BREAD, CAKE & CHOCOLATE

Au Levin du Marais
The patient punters waiting outside this neighbourhood boulangerie in the Marais know exactly where to find the best baguettes in the quartier, as well as wonderful speciality breads and delicious pastries with seasonal fruits.

✉ **32 rue de Turenne, 3e (5, E8)** ☎ 01 42 78 07 31 Ⓜ St-Paul
🕓 Mon-Sat 7am-8pm

Cacao et Chocolat
Here's a contemporary exotic take on choccy, showcasing the bean in all its seductive guises, both solid and liquid. The added citrus notes, spices and even chilli are guaranteed to tease you back for more.

✉ **29 rue du Buci, 6e (5, A3)** ☎ 01 46 33 77 63 Ⓜ Mabillon
🕓 Tues-Sat 10.30am-7.30pm

Dalloyau
The 5 branches around Paris of this venerable pâtisserie (established in 1802) fuel the desire for some of Paris' best croissants, *pain aux raisins*, chocolates and other sinful goodies.

✉ **101 rue du Faubourg St-Honoré,**
8e (3, B5) ☎ 01 42 99 90 00 Ⓜ St-Philippe du Roule 🕓 8.30am-9pm

Jadis et Gourmande
One of 4 branches of shops selling chocolate, chocolate and more chocolate in every conceivable shape and size, plus cocoa from around the world and novelty items like chocolate postcards.

✉ **88 blvd de Port Royal, 5e (3, K9)** ☎ 01 43 26 17 75 Ⓜ Port Royal 🕓 Mon-Sat 1-7pm

Poilâne
Truly a legend in his own lunchtime, Lionel Poilâne bakes perfect wholegrain bread using traditional sourdough leavening and sea salt. Every loaf is an original, but they're all delicious. Pain Poilâne is also available from selected outlets throughout Paris.

✉ **8 rue du Cherche-Midi, 6e (3, G8)**
☎ 01 45 48 42 59
Ⓜ St-Sulpice; Sèvres Babylone 🕓 Mon-Sat 7.15am-8.15pm

Veronica Garbutt

Eeny, meeny, miney mo ...

FOR CHILDREN

Chantelivre

Chantelivre is a bookshop for and about children, with a reasonably good English-language selection. The range includes picture books, novels and videos as well as child psychology and parenting tomes. There's also a play area for nonbrowsing anklebiters.
✉ 13 rue de Sèvres, 6e (3, G8) ☎ 01 45 48 87 90 Ⓜ Sèvres Babylone ⏰ Mon-Sat 10am-7pm (Mon from 1pm)

Le Ciel est à Tout le Monde

If it flies – or looks like it might – you're bound to find it here: kites, boomerangs and frisbees abound. And there's an extraordinary range of toys and dolls (including Babar and Petit Prince ranges) and a bunch of other fun stuff.
✉ 10 rue Gay Lussac, 5e (5, D2) ☎ 01 46 33 21 10 Ⓡ RER Luxembourg ⏰ Mon-Sat 10am-7pm

Du Pareil au Même

The dozen or so branches of this chain offer colourful, fun and durable no-nonsense children's clothing at very reasonable prices.
✉ 122 rue du Faubourg St-Antoine, 12e (2, F12) ☎ 01 43 44 47 66 Ⓜ Ledru Rollin ⏰ Mon-Sat 10am-7pm

FNAC Junior

This kid-oriented branch of the huge FNAC retail chain does everything right with its excellent selection of books, videos, CD-ROMs and educational toys – including letting kids actually play with them. There are organised activities (usually on Wednesday & Saturday), including multi-media playstations, storytelling and puppet shows.
✉ 19 rue Vavin, 6e (3, J8) ☎ 01 56 24 03 46 Ⓜ Vavin ⏰ Mon-Sat 10am-7.30pm

Pom d'Api

Fun, colourful and strong shoes for young feet up to size 40. There's also a range of kids' chairs in the shape of animals.
✉ 13 rue du Jour, 1er (3, D11) ☎ 01 42 36 08 87 Ⓜ Châtelet Les Halles ⏰ Mon-Sat 10.30am-7pm

Si Tu Veux

Imaginative and creative activities for kids, most sold in kit form, plus costumes and traditional toys.
✉ 68 Galerie Vivienne, 2e (3, D10) ☎ 01 42 60 59 97 Ⓜ Bourse ⏰ Mon-Sat 10.30am-7pm

Plenty of trash and perhaps some treasure at a roadside brocante

FLEA MARKETS

Paris' *marchés aux puces* (flea markets), easily accessible by metro, can be great fun if you're in the mood to browse for unexpected treasures among the *brocante* (second-hand goods) and bric-a-brac on display. Some new goods are also available, and a bit of bargaining is expected.

Marché aux Puces de Montreuil (2, F15)
Established in the 19th century, this market is in the south-eastern corner of the 20e, between the Porte de Montreuil metro stop and the ring road. It is known for having good-quality second-hand clothes and designer seconds. The 500 stalls also sell engravings, jewellery, linen, crockery, old furniture and appliances
⊠ **ave de la Porte de Montreuil, 20e Ⓜ Porte de Montreuil** ⊘ **Sat-Mon 7am-7pm**

Marché aux Puces de St-Ouen (2, A9)
This vast flea market, founded in the late 19th century and said to be Europe's largest, is at the northern edge of the 18e

arrondissement. The 2000-odd stalls are grouped into 9 *marchés* (market areas), each with its own specialities (antiques, cheap clothing etc). While shopping, watch out for pickpockets.
⊠ **rue des Rosiers, ave Michelet, rue Voltaire, rue Paul Bert & rue Jean-Henri Fabre, 18e (off Map 3) Ⓜ Porte de Clignancourt** ⊘ **Sat-Mon 7.30am-7pm**

Marché aux Puces de la Porte de Vanves (2, J7) This market in the far south-western corner of the 14e arrondissement is known for its fine selection of junk. Ave Georges Lafenestre looks like a giant car-boot sale, with lots of 'curios' which aren't quite old (or classy)

enough to qualify as antiques. Ave Marc Sangnier is lined with stalls selling new clothes, shoes, handbags and household items.
⊠ **ave Georges Lafenestre & ave Marc Sangnier, 14e Ⓜ Porte de Vanves** ⊘ **Sat-Sun 7am-6pm**

Marché d'Aligre (2, G12) Small but more central than Paris' other 3 flea markets, this market is one of the best places in Paris to rummage through cardboard boxes filled with old clothes and one-of-a-kind accessories worn decades ago by fashionable (and not-so-fashionable) Parisians.
⊠ **Place d'Aligre, 12e Ⓜ Ledru Rollin** ⊘ **Tues-Sun early-1pm**

LATE-NIGHT BUYS

Paris is not a 24-hour city, and shops often close just minutes before you run out of something essential – like chocolate. Here's a few addresses to try when you're desperate.

Boulangerie de l'Ancienne Comédie
Bread and pastries, snacks and sandwiches.
⊠ **10 rue de l'Ancienne Comédie, 6e (5, B3)** ☎ **01 43 26 89 72 Ⓜ Odéon** ⊘ **24hrs**

Drugstore Publicis
Newspapers, books, cigarettes and bits & pieces.
⊠ **131 ave des Champs Élysées, 8e (3,**

B3) ☎ **01 44 43 79 00 Ⓜ Charles de Gaulle-Étoile** ⊘ **10am-2am**

News Kiosque
Newspapers and magazines.
⊠ **Place Charles de Gaulle, 8e (3, B3) Ⓜ Charles de Gaulle-Étoile** ⊘ **24hrs**

Prisunic
For all your supermarket needs.

⊠ **109 rue de la Boétie, 8e (3, B4)** ☎ **01 53 77 65 65 Ⓜ Franklin D Roosevelt** ⊘ **Mon-Sat 9am-midnight**

Shell Garage
Petrol, drinks, sweets and snacks.
⊠ **6 blvd Raspail, 7e (3, F8)** ☎ **01 45 48 43 12 Ⓜ Rue du Bac** ⊘ **24hrs**

SPECIALIST STORES

One of the joys of shopping in Paris is the unexpected boutiques specialising in arcane products or arts.

Anna Joliet

This wonderful little shop specialises in music boxes, both new and old, for romantics and children alike. Just open the door and see if you aren't tempted in.
⊠ **9 rue de Beaujolais, 1er (3, D10)** ☎ **01 42 96 55 13** Ⓜ **Pyramides** ◯ Mon-Sat 10am-7pm

Au Vieux Campeur

This camping chain has 17 shops in the Latin Quarter just east of rue St-Jacques between blvd St-Germain and rue des Écoles. Each specialises in equipment for a specific kind of outdoor activity: hiking, mountaineering, cycling, skiing, snowboarding, scuba diving etc.
⊠ **48 rue des Écoles, 5e (5, C4)** ☎ **01 43 29 12 32** Ⓜ **Cluny La Sorbonne** ◯ Mon 2-7pm, Tues & Thurs-Fri 10.30am-7.30pm, Wed 10.30am-9pm, Sat 10am-7.30pm

EOL' Modelisme

This shop sells expensive toys for big boys and girls, including every sort of model imaginable – from radio-controlled aircraft to huge wooden yachts. The main shop, right by the metro entrance, has an amazing collection of tiny cars.
⊠ **55, 62 & 70 blvd St-Germain, 5e (5, D4)** ☎ **01 43 54 01 43** Ⓜ **Maubert Mutualité** ◯ Mon-Fri 8am-8pm

Galerie Inard (3, G8)

This gallery sells stunning Aubusson tapestries from the postwar period and imaginative, contemporary glass. You won't get much change from 350,000FF for a medium-sized tapestry by a well-known artist.
⊠ **179 blvd St-Germain, 6e** ☎ **01 45 44 66 88** Ⓜ **St-Germain des Prés** ◯ Tues-Sat 10am-12.30pm & 2-7pm

Il pour l'Homme

Housed in an old paint shop with 19th-century display counters and chests of drawers, 'It for the Man' has, well, everything a man could want or not need – from tie clips and cigar cutters to DIY tools and designer tweezers.
⊠ **209 rue St-Honoré, 1er (3, D8)** ☎ **01 42 60 43 56** Ⓜ **Tuileries** ◯ Mon-Sat 10.30am-7pm

Madeleine Gély

(3, F8) One to head for on a rainy day: if you're in the market for a bespoke cane or umbrella, this shop (founded in 1834) will supply.
⊠ **218 blvd St-Germain, 7e** ☎ **01 42 22 63 35** Ⓜ **St-Germain des Prés** ◯ 9.30am-7pm

Mélodies Graphiques

This shop carries all sorts of items made from exquisite Florentine *papier à cuve* (paper hand-decorated with marbled designs). There are several other fine stationery shops along the same street.
⊠ **10 rue du Pont Louis-Philippe, 4e (5, D6)** ☎ **01 42 74 57 68** Ⓜ **Pont Marie** ◯ 11am-7pm (Sun-Mon from 2pm)

Odimex Paris

This shop sells teapots: little ones, big ones, sophisticated ones, comic ones and very expensive ones.
⊠ **17 rue de l'Odéon, 6e (5, B3)** ☎ **01 46 33 98 96** Ⓜ **Odéon**

Robin des Bois

A shop strictly for environmentalists, this place sells everything and anything made from recycled things – from jewellery to stationery.
⊠ **15 rue Fernand Duval, 4e (5, D7)** ☎ **01 48 04 09 36** Ⓜ **St-Paul** ◯ Mon-Sat 10.30am-7.30pm, Sun 2-7.30pm

Sennelier

If your visit to the Musée d'Orsay left you inspired, drop in at Sennelier to find the source of all those vibrant colours. This artists' colour merchant has been in business for well over a century, and still makes paints using rare pigments, as well as supplying other artists' materials.
⊠ **3 Quai Voltaire, 7e (3, F9)** ☎ **01 42 60 72 15** Ⓜ **St-Germain des Prés** ◯ Mon-Sat 9.30am-6.30pm (Mon from 2pm, Tues-Fri closed 12.30-2pm)

places to eat

Food and eating are consuming passions for Parisians. An amazing amount of time is spent thinking and talking about food, with seemingly endless discussions about the merits of this particular restaurant or that particular dish. If you can read French, snaffle a copy of Lonely Planet's *Restoguide Paris*, which reviews hundreds of Paris' best restaurants, cafes and bars.

Cuisine

While many people think of a single 'French cuisine', the truth is there are many, each based on the produce and gastronomy of the individual regions of the country. Fortunately, in Paris, you can sample them all.

You can also feast on an exceptional variety of ethnic food, brought to Paris by successive waves of immigrants from France's former colonies and protectorates in Africa, Indochina, the Middle East, India, the Caribbean and the South Pacific, as well as refugees from every corner of the globe.

The French *petit déjeuner*

Price Ranges

The price ranges used in this chapter indicate the average cost of a 3-course meal for one person ordered à la carte (excluding alcohol).

$	under 125FF
$$	125–200FF
$$$	200–350FF
$$$$	over 350FF

Simon Bracken

Summer plums

(breakfast) often consists of nothing more than a strong black *café*, though a croissant, a light bread roll with jam, or a boiled egg might be added. For many people, lunch is still the main meal of the day. Dinner usually begins around 8.30pm.

Where to Eat

The quintessential Parisian place to eat is the *bistro*, which is usually a small neighbourhood restaurant open just for lunch (12-2pm) and dinner (7.30-10.30pm), and offering a variety of meals *à la carte* or cheaper set-price *menus* (see p. 81). Bistros often specialise in the food of a particular region.

Brasseries have their roots in Alsatian beer halls. They are often large places serving meals at all times of the day, often traditional fare such as *choucroute*, oysters, and steak and *frites* (chips).

The cafe is an important focal point for social life, and sitting in one to read, write, talk with friends or merely watch the world go by is an integral part of many Parisians' day-to-day existence. Only basic food (sandwiches, salads) is available in most cafes.

Alcoholic drinks are available wherever you eat, or at cafes even if you don't eat. You'll usually pay 20-25FF for a glass of beer or decent wine in a cafe. Wine with meals generally starts at around 85FF a bottle, with most being in the 100-150FF range; 250FF will get you a fine drop indeed.

LOUVRE & LES HALLES

The area between the Forum des Halles and the Centre Pompidou (1er and western 4e) is filled with scores of *branché* ('plugged-in', or trendy) restaurants. Streets with places to eat include rue des Lombards, bar and bistro-lined rue Montorgueil, and the narrow streets north and east of Forum des Halles.

Angelina $$
French
Angelina's is where Louvre-weary tourists bump shoulders with trendy shoppers and coiffed matrons. It's true that some do partake of tea or munch a salad or sandwich, but the real reason they congregate here is the hot chocolate to die for.
✉ **226 rue de Rivoli, 1er (3, D8)** ☎ **01 42 60 82 00; fax 01 42 86 98 97** Ⓜ **Tuileries** ◷ **Mon-Fri 9am-7pm, Sat-Sun 9am-7.30pm** Ⓥ

Au Pied de Cochon $$$
French
This big, bright and bustling all-nighter made its name filling the bellies of Les Halles porters and theatre-goers alike. Now it's tourists and night owls tucking in to the filling traditional fare: *pied de cochon* (pig's trotter) and other pork dishes, onion soup, year-round

Café Marly

oysters and huge seafood platters. Lunch *menu* 146FF.
✉ **6 rue Coquillière, 1er (3, D10)** ☎ **01 40 13 77 00** Ⓜ **Châtelet Les Halles** ◷ **24hrs**

Café Marly $$$
Modern French
Sipping something cool under the colonnades of the Louvre, overlooking the glowing pyramid on a warm spring evening ... this is about as good as it gets in this life. The Marly serves fresh and contemporary fare, tending towards white meats, fish and salad, with a great fruit salad to finish. Bookings advisable.
✉ **93 rue de Rivoli, 1er**

(3, E9) ☎ **01 46 26 06 60** Ⓜ **Palais Royal** ◷ **restaurant: 11am-1am; bar: 8am-2am**

Isse $$$$
Japanese
A piece of Tokyo's Ginza has been magically transported to the heart of Paris, with quality and service (and prices) intact. In this modern blonde-wood setting, populated by art and finance types, you'll find irreproachable sushi and sashimi, delicious grilled eel and delicate tempura. Bookings advisable. Lunch *menu* 150FF.
✉ **56 rue Ste-Anne, 1er (3, D9)** ☎ **01 42 96 67 76; fax 01 42 96 82 63** Ⓜ **Pyramides; Quatre Septembre** ◷ **lunch Tues-Fri 12-2pm, dinner Tues-Sat 7-10pm**

Joe Allen $$
American
Friendly American bar/restaurant with great atmosphere and a good selection of Californian wines. Snack on buffalo wings or tuck into a grilled half chicken with barbecue sauce, baked potato and coleslaw. Sunday brunch is 12-4pm. *Menu* 112/140FF.
✉ **30 rue Pierre Lescot, 1er (5, A7)** ☎ **01 42 36 70 13** Ⓜ **Étienne Marcel** ◷ **noon-2am**

Tipping & Taxes
By law, all cafes, bars and restaurants include a 15% service charge (*service compris*) in your bill, making it unnecessary to tip; but by all means leave a little extra on the table for exceptional service.

Karine Ioannou–Sophoclis

MARAIS & ST-PAUL

The Marais (4e and southern 3e), filled with small eateries of every imaginable kind, is one of Paris' premier neighbourhoods for eating out. The pretty little Place du Marché Ste-Catherine (5, E7) is surrounded by small restaurants – a bit pricey, but you're paying for the pleasant outdoor location.

404 $$$
Moroccan
The 404 has some of the best couscous and *tajine* in Paris. It also has excellent grills and tasty aniseed bread. The restaurant – done up like the inside of an old Moroccan home – is owned by the French-Arab comedian Smaïn, so the atmosphere is always upbeat. The Sunday *brunch berbère* (Berber brunch) is recommended. Bookings essential. Lunch *menu* 89FF, weekend brunch *menu* 125FF.
✉ **69 rue des Gravilliers, 3e (5, A8)**
☎ **01 42 74 57 81**
Ⓜ **Arts et Métiers**
⏲ **lunch 12-2.30pm (Sat-Sun to 4pm), dinner 8pm-midnight**

Amadeo $$
Modern French
This chic Mozart-mad restaurant is decidedly gay, although straight diners are also very welcome. The food is stylish and delicious. A highlight is the live opera or operetta performance held on the first Thursday of each month, with a special *prix fixe menu* to match. Bookings essential. Lunch *menu* 75/95FF.
✉ **19 rue François Miron, 4e (5, D7)**
☎ **01 48 87 01 02**
Ⓜ **St-Paul; Hôtel de Ville** ⏲ **weekdays lunch and dinner, Saturday dinner**

Café Beaubourg $$
French
This minimalist cafe opposite the Centre Pompidou draws in an arty crowd, and there's always free entertainment on the large square in front. Sunday brunch on the terrace is highly recommended.
✉ **100 rue St-Martin, 1er (5, B7)** ☎ **01 48 87 63 96; fax 01 48 87 81 25** Ⓜ **Châtelet Les Halles** ⏲ **Mon-Fri 8am-1am, Sat-Sun 8am-2am**

Chez Marianne $$
Kosher
A Sephardic (Middle Eastern/North African Jewish) alternative to the nearby Ashkenazic (Eastern European Jewish) Jo Goldenberg, this restaurant/deli/takeaway specialises in *mezze* (felafel, hummus, meatballs etc), as well as honey-oozing baklava. Bookings advisable. *Menu* 55/75FF.
✉ **2 rue des Hospitalières St-Gervais, 4e (5, D7)** ☎ **01 42 72 18 86** Ⓜ **St-Paul** ⏲ **noon-midnight**

Chez Robert et Louise $$
French
This authentic country inn – complete with red gingham curtains – offers delightful, unfussy and inexpensive French food prepared by a husband and wife team. Dishes include *côte de bœuf* cooked on an open fire. Bookings advisable.
✉ **64 rue Vieille du Temple, 3e (5, C8)**
☎ **01 42 78 55 89** Ⓜ **St-Sébastien Froissart** ⏲ **Mon-Sat lunch 12-2.30pm, dinner 7-10pm**

Les Chimères $
French
Open around the clock, this amazing place seems to change with the hour. There's something for everyone, with traditional daily specials, raw salmon tartare or exotic tapas. In the evenings it transforms magically into an Australian pub. *Menu* 58FF.
✉ **133 rue St-Antoine, 4e (5, E7)** ☎ **01 42 72 71 97** Ⓜ **St-Paul** ⏲ **24hrs**

L'Enoteca $$$
Italian
Great Italian food in the lovely Village St-Paul. Risotto with gorgonzola and pears, tagliatelle with prawns and asparagus, and carpaccio with rocket are among the favourites. There's also a list of over 300 excellent Italian wines. Bookings advisable. Lunch *menu* 100FF.
✉ **25 rue Charles V, 4e (5, E7)** ☎ **01 42 78 91 44** Ⓜ **Pont Marie** ⏲ **lunch Mon-Fri 12-2pm, dinner Mon-Sat 7.30-10.30pm**

Ma Bourgogne $$$
French
Overlooking Place des Vosges, Ma Bourgogne is one of the few Parisian restaurants where you can eat on the terrace morning, noon and night 7 days a week. *Menu* 195FF.
✉ **19 Place des Vosges, 4e (5, E8)** ☎ **01 42 78 44 64; fax 01 42 78 19 37** Ⓜ **St-Paul; Bastille** ⏲ **8am-1.30am**

Pitchi Poï $$
Polish
This Eastern European Jewish restaurant beamed down onto a picturesque little square on the edge of the Marais will warm the cockles with its trademark *tchoulent* (slow-simmered duck with vegetables) or *datcha* (smoked salmon served with a baked spud and cream). And of course

Simon Bracken

there's chopped liver and strudel. Bookings advisable for dinner. *Menu* 119FF.
✉ **7 Place du Marché Ste-Catherine, 4e (5, E7)** ☎ **01 42 77 46 15** Ⓜ **St-Paul** ⏲ **lunch 12-2.30pm, dinner 7.30-11pm** ⚓

Le Valet de Carreau $$
French
This neighbourhood restaurant justifiably attracts a loyal following with dishes like charlotte of salmon and duck galette (described by one wag as 'nouvelle cuisine with quantity') followed by the house speciality, *moelleux au chocolat*. But the main drawcard is undoubtedly the wonderful terrace under the chestnut trees. Bookings advisable. *Menu* 75/180FF.
✉ **2 rue Dupetit-Thouars, 3e (5, B10)** ☎ **01 42 72 72 60; fax 01 42 72 71 71** Ⓜ **Temple; République** ⏲ **lunch Mon-Fri 12-2.30pm, dinner Mon-Sat 8-10.30pm**

ÎLE ST-LOUIS

Famed for its ice cream as much as anything else, the Île St-Louis (4e) is generally an expensive place to eat. It's best suited to those looking for a light snack or the finest ingredients for lunch beside the Seine.

Brasserie de l'Île St-Louis $$
Alsatian
Founded in 1870, this spectacularly situated brasserie features *choucroute garnie* (sauerkraut

with assorted prepared meats) and other Alsatian dishes, but you can also enjoy the location by just ordering coffee or a mug of beer. Bookings advisable.
✉ **55 quai de Bourbon,**

4e (5, D6) ☎ **01 43 54 02 59** Ⓜ **Pont Marie** ⏲ **Thurs-Tues 11.30am-1am (Thurs from 5pm)**

Les Fous de L'Île $$
French
An exception to the touristy nature of the Île St-Louis, this friendly and down-to-earth establishment serves reasonably priced light lunches and meals. Bookings advisable.
✉ **33 rue des Deux Ponts, 4e (5, E6)** ☎ **01 43 25 76 67** Ⓜ **Pont Marie** ⏲ **Tues-Fri 12-11pm, Sat 3-11pm, Sun 12-7pm**

Noshing with Nippers

Unfortunately, French restaurants have yet to cotton onto the fact that children are diners too. Most restaurants don't have highchairs, children's menus or children's portions. In fact, children are rarely seen in most Parisian restaurants – which may help explain the popularity of the American chain restaurants and their French counterparts (such as Hippopotamus) which specifically cater to parents with kids in tow.

QUARTIER LATIN

Rue Mouffetard (5, E3) in the 5e is filled with scores of places to eat. It's especially popular with students, in part because of the unparalleled selection of stands selling baguette sandwiches, *panini* (Italian toasted bread with fillings) and crêpes. Rue Soufflot (5, D3) is lined with cafes.

Le Fogon St-Julien $$$
Spanish

The real treat here is the authentic paella, including saffron, vegetable, rabbit, chicken or seafood. But the best is the *arroz negro*, black with squid ink hiding chunks of fish and shrimp. Bookings advisable. *Menu 90/120/175FF.*

✉ 10 rue St-Julien-le-Pauvre, 5e (5, C5)
☎ 01 43 54 31 33; fax 01 43 54 07 00
Ⓜ Maubert Mutualité; St-Michel ☺ Mon-Sat lunch 12-4pm, dinner 7.40pm-2am

Jardin des Pâtes $
Italian

Not far from the Jardin des Plantes, the cosy 'Garden of Pastas' has as many types of pasta as you care to name (wholewheat, buckwheat, chestnut etc), all made from 100% *biologique* (natural) stone-ground grains. The dishes are simple and filling. Wine by the glass and excellent fresh juices are available. Bookings advisable for dinner.

✉ 4 rue Lacépède, 5e (3, J12) ☎ 01 43 31 50 71 Ⓜ Cardinal Lemoine ☺ lunch 12-2.30pm, dinner 7-11pm Ⓥ

Moissonnier $$$
Lyonnais

Hearty Lyon-inspired cuisine has been served at this elegant restaurant since 1960, including quenelles (a kind of fish dumpling), *saladier Lyonnais* (a selection of appetisers including fresh greens, bacon, eggs and anchovies), *boudin noir* (black pudding) and tripe. Bookings advisable. *Menu 150FF.*

✉ 28 rue des Fossés St-Bernard, 5e (5, E5)
☎ 01 43 29 87 65
Ⓜ Cardinal Lemoine ☺ lunch Tues-Sun 12-1.30pm, dinner Tues-Sat 7-9.30pm

Restaurant du Hammam de la Mosquée $
Moroccan

The restaurant at this authentic – and very atmospheric – mosque and hammam serves the usual complement of tajines and couscous. For the complete experience, the *formule orientale* includes use of the hammam and a massage plus

a meal for 300FF. Bookings advisable.
✉ 39 rue Geoffroy St-Hilaire, 5e (3, K13)
☎ 01 43 32 18 14; fax 01 43 31 53 30
✉ nour-l@wanadoo.fr
Ⓜ Place Monge ☺ lunch 12.30-3pm, dinner 7.30-10.30pm

> **Meal Freebies**
> Bread (normally a sliced baguette) is provided free of charge with meals. You will normally need to ask for water (*une carafe d'eau*), which is also free of charge.

Instant indigestion in the Quartier Latin

ODÉON & ST-GERMAIN

Rue St-André des Arts (5, B4) is lined with restaurants, including a few down the covered passage between Nos 59 and 61. There are lots of places between Église St-Sulpice and Église St-Germain des Prés (5, A3), especially along rue des Canettes, rue Princesse and rue Guisarde.

Chez Albert $$$
Portuguese
Authentic Portuguese food is not easy to come by in Paris, but this friendly family-run place has it in spades: *cataplana* (pork with clams), numerous *bacalhau* (dried cod) dishes and prawns sautéed in lots of garlic, plus a good selection of Portuguese wines. Bookings advisable. *Menu* 90/135FF.
✉ **43 rue Mazarine, 6e (5, A4)** ☎ **01 46 33 22 57** Ⓜ **Odéon** ⏱ **lunch Tues-Sat 12-2.30pm, dinner Mon-Sat 7-11pm**

Coffee Parisien $
American
This cafe/diner offers something of a détente in the burger-chain wars. Surrounded by Ameri-kitsch and under the ever-present eye of JFK, shining, happy people munch commendable cheeseburgers, club sandwiches, Caesars and other snacky offerings late into the night.
✉ **4 rue Princesse, 6e (5, A3)** ☎ **01 43 54 18 18** Ⓜ **Mabillon** ⏱ **11.30am-midnight**

Cour de Rohan $$
French
Local writers and publishers seek peace, quiet and home-made scones in this slightly faded tearoom, with its assortment of exquisite furniture and *objets*. Mixed salads and daily specials complement the aromatic teas, while 3 pastry chefs keep the dessert cart piled with delicious delicacies.
✉ **59-61 rue St-André des Arts, 6e (5, B4)** ☎ **01 43 25 79 67** Ⓜ **Mabillon; Odéon** ⏱ **12-7.30pm (Sat-Sun to 11pm)** Ⓥ

Jacques Cagna $$$$
French
In his 17th-century mansion hung with Flemish masters, Jacques Cagna continues his mastery of original *haute cuisine* – *filet de bœuf poêlé aux truffes de Périgord* or escalope of veal sweetbreads with crayfish and fresh coriander lasagne. The 260FF lunch *menu* (470FF dinner) is a fine introduction to the man's talents. Bookings advisable.

✉ **14 rue des Grands Augustins, 6e (5, B4)** ☎ **01 43 26 49 39/** ☎ **01 43 54 54 48** Ⓜ **Mabillon; Odéon** ⏱ **lunch Tues-Fri 12-2pm, dinner Mon-Sat 7.30-10.30pm**

Le Petit Zinc $$$
French
This wonderful (and expensive) place serves regional specialities from the south-west of France (the signature calf's liver is sublime) in mock-Art Nouveau splendour. Bookings advisable. *Menu* 168FF.
✉ **11 rue St-Benoît, 6e (3, F9)** ☎ **01 42 61 20 60** Ⓜ **St-Germain des Prés** ⏱ **noon-2am**

Polidor $
French
Lunch at this very cosy *crêmerie-restaurant* is a trip back to Victor Hugo's Paris – the restaurant and its decor date from 1845. The inexpensive *menus* (55/100FF) of tasty, family-style French cuisine attract students, locals and tourists alike. Specialities include the most famous *tarte tatin* (caramelised apple pie) in Paris. Cash only.
✉ **41 rue Monsieur-le-Prince, 6e (5, C3)** ☎ **01 43 26 95 34** Ⓜ **Odéon** ⏱ **lunch 12-2.30pm, dinner 7pm-12.30am (Sun to 11pm)**

Les Deux Cafes
Side by side on blvd St-Germain sit the *Deux Magots* (No 170) and *Café de Flore* (No 172), once the canteens of bohemian artists and writers such as Jean-Paul Sartre, Simone de Beauvoir and Albert Camus. Today they cater for a more prosaic clientele, but their terraces are still a good spot to watch the passing parade.

CHAMPS ÉLYSÉES

Few places along touristy ave des Champs Élysées offer good value, but some of the restaurants in the surrounding area are excellent.

Apicius **$$$$**
French
Owner/chef Jean-Pierre Vigato is acclaimed for his fine and subtle dishes. Don't go past the foie gras *classique Apicius* in a sweet & sour confit of horseradish. Follow with spit-roasted calf's sweetbread and celeriac simmered with truffles or the wonderful medley of 5 fish. Bookings advisable; smart dress.
✉ **122 ave de Villiers, 17e (2, C6)** ☎ **01 43 80 19 66** Ⓜ **Péreire**
◷ **Mon-Fri lunch 12-2pm, dinner 8-10pm**

Asian **$$**
Asian
Good Asian cooking is still something of a rarity in Paris, but talented chef Oth Sambath has found plenty of converts to his fresh and piquant style, with influences ranging from Thai to Japanese. Bookings advisable. Lunch *menu* 98FF.
✉ **30 ave George V, 8e (3, C3)** ☎ **01 56 89 11 00; fax 01 56 89 11 01** ℮ **www.asiancompany.com** Ⓜ **George V**
◷ **12-2pm**

Le Bistrot du Sommelier **$$$$**
French
This the Parisian restaurant *sans pareil* for wine buffs. Philippe Faure-Brac was named Meilleur Sommelier du Monde in 1992, and the *dégustation menus* offer his hand-picked selection of *crus* by-the-glass matched with some canny

cooking. Bookings essential; smart dress. *Menu* 390/480/650FF.
✉ **97 blvd Haussmann, 8e (3, A6)** ☎ **01 42 65 24 85** Ⓜ **St-Augustin**
◷ **Mon-Fri lunch 12-2.30pm, dinner 7.30-11pm**

Flora Danica **$$$**
Scandinavian
Just a few steps away from the bustle of the Champs Élysées is a quiet little terrace with a Nordic cast. Danish salmon is the speciality of the house, appearing in a multitude of guises: marinated, grilled, pickled or even fondue. Or try the reindeer fillets with wild berries – and try not to think of Christmas. Bookings advisable; smart dress. *Menu* 175FF.
✉ **142 ave des Champs Élysées, 8e (3, B3)** ☎ **01 44 13 86 26; fax 01 42 25 83 10** ℮ **www.restaurant.copenhage.com** Ⓜ **Charles de Gaulle-Étoile**
◷ **lunch 12-2.30pm, dinner 7.15-11pm**

Ladurée **$$$**
French
The salons of this sumptuous *belle époque* tearoom, established in 1862, are named after the mistresses of Napoleon III: Mathilde, Castiglione and Paeva. But it's difficult to imagine any of them being as sweet as the pastries Ladurée is famous for. Mixed salads and light lunches round out the menu. Bookings advisable. Dinner *menu* 195FF.

✉ **75 ave des Champs Élysées, 8e (3, B4)** ☎ **01 40 75 08 75; fax 01 40 75 00 50** Ⓜ **George V** ◷ **7.30am-1am** Ⓥ

Maison Prunier **$$$$**
Seafood
This venerable fish and seafood restaurant, founded in 1925, is famed for its over-the-top Art Deco interior, as well as for its oysters and market-fresh catches of the day. Finish at the bar with one of a selection of vintage rums from Martinique. Book at least 2 days ahead.
✉ **16 ave Victor Hugo, 16e (3, B2)** ☎ **01 44 17 35 85; fax 01 44 17 90 10** Ⓜ **Charles de Gaulle-Étoile** ◷ **lunch Tues-Sat 12-3pm, dinner Mon-Sat 7.30-11pm**

Spoon Food & Wine **$$$**
International
Michelin 3-star (twice!) chef Alain Ducasse invites diners to mix & match their own mains and sauces: do you prefer satay, curry or Béarnaise sauce with your grilled calamari? Controversially, the cellar features wines from the USA, Australia and Europe, with only a small proportion being French. Bookings advisable.
✉ **14 rue de Marignan, 8e (3, C4)** ☎ **01 40 76 34 44; fax 01 40 76 34 37** ℮ **www.spoon .tm.fr** Ⓜ **Franklin D Roosevelt** ◷ **Mon-Fri lunch 12-3pm, dinner 7pm-midnight**

GRANDS BOULEVARDS

This area, encompassing part of the 2e and 9e, has a number of fine restaurants worth trying. Neon-lit blvd du Montmartre (3, B10) and nearby parts of rue du Faubourg Montmartre (neither of which are anywhere near the neighbourhood of Montmartre) form one of Paris' most animated cafe and dining districts.

Haynes Restaurant $$
American
This legendary and very funky be-bop and beat-generation hangout dishes up genuine gumbo, fried and barbecue chicken, cornbread, and divine burgers. There's usually a lively crowd for the jazz sessions on Friday & Saturday (bookings advisable for dinner).
✉ **3 rue Clauzel, 9e (3, A10)** ☎ **01 48 78 40 63** Ⓜ **St-Georges** ◷ **Tues-Sat 7pm-12.30am**

Mi Ranchito $$
Colombian
Of all Colombian exports, cuisine must be one of the rarest. In this small, discreet eatery the Andes meets the Antilles, with plantain bananas, avocados, manioc, corn cakes, chilli and coconut milk among the exotic offerings. Dishes are based around chicken, seafood and beef, with some dishes cooked in banana leaves. Bookings advisable. Lunch *menu* 65FF, dinner and weekends 95FF. Children's *menu* 48FF.
✉ **35 rue de Montholon, 9e (3, A11)** ☎ **01 48 78 45 94; fax 01 42 80 95 54** Ⓜ **Cadet** ◷ **lunch Sun-Fri 12-3pm, dinner daily 7pm-midnight** ⚹ **yes**

Wally le Saharien $$$
Morocco
Wally's is a cut above most of the Maghreb restaurants in Paris, offering couscous in its pure Saharan form – without stock or vegetables, just a finely cooked grain served with a delicious sauce. Couscous as it's meant to be. The rich Moorish coffee is a fitting finish. Bookings advisable on Friday & Saturday for dinner.
✉ **36 rue Rodier, 9e (3, A10)** ☎ **01 42 85 51 90** Ⓜ **St-Georges** ◷ **Tues-Sat lunch 12-2.30pm, dinner 7.30-10.30pm** Ⓥ

Je Suis Végétarien

Vegetarians are a near-invisible minority in France and are not well catered for. Exclusively vegetarian restaurants are rare, though many restaurants have at least one vegetarian dish on the menu (but you'll soon get sick of cheese omelettes) and you can get a fresh salad just about anywhere.

Most North African and Middle Eastern restaurants have some meatless dishes on the menu. Better still, there's a handful of Indian restaurants to choose from. **Passage Brady** (3, B13) in the 10e is chock full of sub-continental restaurants and groceries. Elsewhere, **La Ville de Jagannath** (☎ 01 43 55 80 81), 101 rue St-Maur, 11e (2, E12), is a New Age-inspired *thali* spot, while **L'Étoile du Kasmir** (☎ 01 43 55 57 60) at 63 rue de Charonne, 11e (2, F12), does filling, inexpensive thali lunches.

Unfortunately, very few fixed-price *menus* include vegetarian options. A couple of places where vegetarians *can* find a decent meal are:

Aquarius – good-value vegetarian restaurant; see page 82
Le Bol en Bois (☎ 01 47 07 27 24) 35 rue Pascal, 13e (2, H10) – tasty Zen macrobiotic dishes
Jardin des Pâtes – not a vegetarian restaurant, but there's a good selection of meatless dishes on the menu; see page 75
Le Victoire Supréme du Cœur (☎ 01 40 41 93 95) 41 rue des Bourdonnais, 1er (5, A6) – Sri Chimnoy centre serving decent vegetarian fare

BASTILLE & FAUBOURG ST-ANTOINE

This area – mostly the 11e and 12e but also the westernmost part of the 4e – is chock-a-block with restaurants. Narrow, scruffy rue de Lappe (2, F12) may not look like much during the day, but it's one of the trendiest cafe and nightlife streets in Paris, attracting a young, alternative crowd. Many of the places speak with a Spanish accent – Tex-Mex, tapas and Cuban food can all be found here. Things really start to pick up late at night.

Le Bistrot du Dôme $$$
Seafood
This inviting restaurant specialises in superbly prepared seafood dishes. From the flavoursome fish soups to impeccable fish mains (accompanied by a perfectly chosen wine list) and delicious desserts, there's rarely a false note. Bookings essential.
✉ 2 rue de la Bastille, 4e (3, G15) ☎ 01 48 04 88 44 Ⓜ Bastille ⏲ lunch 12.30-2.30pm, dinner 7.30-11.30pm

Blue Elephant $$$
Thai
Paris' most famous Thai restaurant is one of a hip international chain with branches in London and Dubai. While it has become a little too successful for its own good, the indoor tropical rainforest and well-prepared spicy dishes are still worth the inflated prices. Bookings advisable. *Menu* 275FF.
✉ 43 rue de la Roquette, 11e (2, F12) ☎ 01 47 00 42 00 Ⓜ Bastille ⏲ lunch Mon-Fri 12-2.30pm, dinner Mon-Sat 7pm-midnight Ⓥ

Brasserie Bofinger $$$
French
This is reputedly the oldest

Memorable mussels

brasserie in Paris (founded in 1864), with original Art Deco brass, glass and mirrors, and it's still, deservedly, one of the most popular. Specialities include oysters, choucroute and seafood dishes, and the *menu* includes a half-bottle of wine. Bookings advisable for dinner and Sunday lunch. *Menu* 119/178FF.
✉ 5-7 rue de la Bastille, 4e (3, G15) ☎ 01 42 72 87 82 Ⓜ Bastille ⏲ lunch Mon-Fri 12-3pm, dinner 6.30pm-1am, Sat-Sun noon-1am

L'Ébauchoir $$
French
Warm colours, small wooden tables, regular customers and smiling young staff are the first impressions of this convivial little neighbourhood bistro. The carefully prepared food is

typical bistro fare – with a twist of originality: snails or fennel with lemon for starters, followed by veal liver with honey and coriander. Bookings advisable for dinner. Lunch *menu* 68/90FF.
✉ 45 rue de Cîteaux, 12e (2, G12) ☎ 01 43 42 49 31 Ⓜ Faidherbe Chaligny ⏲ Mon-Sat lunch 12-2.30pm, dinner 8-11pm

L'Écailler du Bistrot $$
Seafood
This friendly little place might be a little off the beaten track, but it's worth searching out for its excellent range of fresh seafood, including a wide selection of oysters, grey shrimp, spider crabs, salmon (fresh *rillettes* or smoked *maison*), salt cod and other delicacies of the

deep. Bookings advisable. Lunch *menu* 78FF.
✉ **22 rue Paul-Bert, 11e (2, F13)** ☎ **01 43 72 76 77** Ⓜ **Faidherbe Chaligny** ☺ **lunch Mon-Fri 12-2.30pm, dinner Mon-Sat 7.30-11.30pm**

Lire entre les Vignes $$
Modern French
Hidden away in a nondescript Bastille street, 'Read Between the Vines' is an oasis of conviviality, reminiscent of a comfortable and spacious country kitchen, and a great spot to dine with friends. The food is fresh, imaginative and tasty – prepared before your eyes in the corner kitchen. Bookings advisable.
✉ **38 rue Sedaine, 11e (2, F12)** ☎ **01 43 55 69 49** Ⓜ **Bastille; Bréguet Sabin** ☺ **Mon-Fri lunch 12-2.30pm, dinner 8-10.30pm**

Le Square Trousseau $$
French
This vintage bistro, with its etched glass and polished wood panelling, is comfortable rather than trendy and attracts a mixed clientele, including some brand-name fashion icons. The carefully prepared food is of high quality, but most people come to enjoy the lovely terrace overlooking the eponymous square. Bookings advisable. *Menu* 100/135FF.
✉ **1 rue Antoine Vollon, 12e (2, F12)** ☎ **01 43 43 06 00; fax 01 43 43 00 66** Ⓜ **Ledru Rollin** ☺ **lunch 11.30am-2pm, dinner 7-10.30pm**

Suds $$
International
No, not a trendy laundrette but a very branché bar-restaurant with a name that means 'Souths', and with jazz or Latin music in the basement. The cuisine here is anything and everything from the south – from Mexican and Peruvian to Portuguese and North African. Bookings required. Lunch *menu* 70FF.
✉ **55 rue de Charonne, 11e (2, F12)** ☎ **01 43 14 06 36; fax 01 44 83 05 34** Ⓜ **Ledru Rollin; Bastille** ☺ **lunch Tues-Fri 12-2pm, dinner Tues-Sun 8pm-2am**

Swann & Vincent $$
Italian
This open, light and friendly place offers great Italian food: tasty home-style breads, antipasto, a choice of pasta or meat mains, tiramisu and Italian wines. Bookings advisable. Weekday lunch *menu* 82FF.
✉ **7 rue St-Nicolas, 12e (2, F12)** ☎ **01 43 43 49 40** Ⓜ **Ledru Rollin** ☺ **lunch 12-2.45pm, dinner 7.30pm-midnight** **V**

OBERKAMPF & BELLEVILLE

The northern part of the 11e, east of Place de la République, and the 20e along rue Oberkampf and its extension, rue de Ménilmontant, are increasingly popular with diners and denizens of the night. Rue de Belleville (2, D13) is dotted with Chinese, Vietnamese and Turkish places, and blvd de Belleville has loads of kosher couscous restaurants (closed on Saturday).

Au Trou Normand $
French
This very French, cosy little canteen is famous for having some of the lowest prices in Paris. Diners sit at shared, plastic-covered tables, swigging house red from Pyrex glasses and tucking into simple but copious mounds of food. Mains are mostly meat with home-made frites.
✉ **9 rue Jean-Pierre Timbaud, 11e (2, E12)** ☎ **01 48 05 80 23** Ⓜ **Oberkampf** ☺ **Mon-Sat lunch 12-2.30pm, dinner 7.30-11.30pm**

Le Baratin $$
French
This animated wine bistro, just a step away from a stunning vista over Paris and the lively Belleville quartier, offers some of the best food in the 20e. The wine selection (by the glass or carafe) is excellent. Bookings advisable. Weekday lunch *menu* 73FF.
✉ **3 rue Jouye-Rouve, 20e (2, D13)** ☎ **01 43 49 39 70** Ⓜ **Belleville** ☺ **restaurant: Tues-Sat lunch 12-3pm, dinner 8pm-midnight; bar: noon-2am**

Le Charbon $
French
With its remarkable dis-

tressed-retro-industrial ambience, the Charbon was the first – and many opine the best – of the hip new cafes and bars to sprout up in Ménilmontant. Its cocktail of frenetic cool, inexpensive *plats du jour* and evening DJ or live music still hit the spot.
✉ 109 rue Oberkampf, 11e (2, E12) ☎ 01 43 57 55 13 Ⓜ Parmentier ⏰ 9am-2am

Krung Thep   S
Thai
Considered by many to be the most authentic Thai restaurant in Paris, the kitsch 'Bangkok' is a small (some might say cramped) place with favourites like green curries, tom yam gung and fish or chicken steamed in banana leaves. The steamed shrimp ravioli and stuffed crab also hit the spot. Bookings advisable.
✉ 93 rue Julien Lacroix, 20e (2, D12) ☎ 01 43 66 83 74 Ⓜ Belleville ⏰ 6pm-midnight

Le Pavillon Puebla $$$
Catalan
This exquisite Catalan restaurant is housed in a Second Empire pavilion in Buttes Chaumont. The seafood and fish dishes – anchovy tarte, bouillabaisse and cod stuffed with snails – are as attractive as the wonderful terrace (open in summer). For dessert, don't miss the *mille-feuille aux fraises* (strawberries in layers of flaky pastry). Bookings advisable. *Menu* 180/250FF.
✉ Parc des Buttes Chaumont, cnr ave Simon Bolivar and rue Botzaris, 19e (2, C12)

☎ 01 42 08 92 62 Ⓜ Buttes Chaumont ⏰ Tues-Sat lunch 12-2.30pm, dinner 7-10.30pm

La Piragua   S
Colombian
Colombian food and good Latino music feature at this small and friendly restaurant. The fixed-price *menus* are excellent value or choose an à la carte starter like empañadas and fried plantains followed by marinated chicken, cooked with smoked bacon and raisins. Bookings advisable. *Menu* 96/110FF.
✉ 6 rue Rochebrune, 11e (2, E12) ☎ 01 40 21 35 98 Ⓜ St-Ambroise ⏰ Mon-Sat

lunch 12-2pm, dinner 7.30-10.30pm

Le Zéphyr $$
French
Out in the sticks beyond Buttes Chaumont, this elegant 1930s bistro is worth the 8FF metro ride for its refined cooking and genial ambience. A typical *menu* offers eggplant ravioli with mint vinaigrette and roasted lamb noisettes with anchovies and *crème brûlée à la tomate* to finish. Bookings advisable. *Menu* 72/160FF.
✉ 1 rue du Jourdain, 20e (2, D13) ☎ 01 46 36 65 81 Ⓜ Jourdain ⏰ lunch Mon-Fri 12-2.30pm, dinner Mon-Sat 8-11pm

---

Menu v. *Menu*

Most restaurants offer you the choice of ordering à la carte (from the menu) or ordering one fixed-price, multicourse meal known in French as a *menu* or a *formule*. The latter usually has fewer choices but allows you to pick 2 out of 3 courses (eg starter and main course or main course and dessert). A *menu* almost always costs much less than ordering à la carte. Where we have indicated more than 1 *menu* price, the cheaper is normally only available at lunchtime.

Keep in mind that the word 'menu' is one of the 'false friends' of English and French. If you *really* want to see the menu (ie a list of all the dishes available) you ask for *la carte*.

BUTTES AUX CAILLES & CHINATOWN

Dozens of East Asian restaurants line the main streets of Paris' Chinatown (13e), including ave de Choisy and ave d'Ivry (2, J11). But there are a couple of French options too. The cheapest *menus*, which go for about 50FF, are usually available only at lunch on weekdays.

L'Avant-Goût **$$**
Modern French
In this prototype of the Parisian 'neo-bistro', chef Christophe Beaufront serves some of the most inventive modern cuisine around (courgette stuffed with fresh goat's cheese, lamb confit with rosemary and polenta, fig & apple tart). Bookings essential. *Menu* 59/145FF.
✉ 26 rue Bobillot, 13e (2, J10) ☎ 01 53 80 24 00; fax 01 53 80 00 77 Ⓜ Place d'Italie ⏲ Tues-Sat lunch 12-2pm, dinner 8-11pm

Le Temps des Cérises **$**
French
The relaxed atmosphere of this 'anarchistic' restaurant run by a workers' cooperative, together with the good solid fare (rabbit with mustard, steak frites) and especially the low prices, keep regulars coming back for more. It's always packed and the atmosphere is great. *Menu* 58/78/118FF.
✉ 18-20 rue de la Buttes aux Cailles, 13e (2, J10) ☎ 01 45 89 69 48 Ⓜ Corvisart ⏲ lunch Mon-Fri 11.45am-2.15pm, dinner Mon-Sat 7.30-11.45pm

MONTPARNASSE

Since the 1920s, the area around blvd du Montparnasse (6e and 14e) has been one of the city's premier avenues for enjoying that most Parisian of pastimes: sitting in a cafe and checking out the passers-by.

Al Wady **$$**
Lebanese
'The Valley' is the favourite restaurant of many Lebanese Parisians, especially those craving the flavours of the mountains. The carefully prepared banquet-style *mezze* are fresh and flavoursome: make sure you try the delicious *frakeh* (lamb with crushed wheat and spices). Bookings advisable.
✉ 153 rue de Lourmel, 15e (2, H5) ☎ 01 45 58 57 18; fax 01 47 94 19 47 ✉ zeina@club internet.fr Ⓜ Lourmel ⏲ lunch 11am-3pm, dinner 7pm-midnight

Aquarius **$**
Vegetarian
The best of Paris' few vegetarian restaurants, Aquarius offers an imaginative and filling range of dishes for both committed vegans and vegos as well as those simply craving something a little less 'sophisticated' than much French cuisine. There's a second Aquarius (☎ 01 48 87 48 71) at 54 rue Ste-Croix de la Bretonnerie, 4e (5, C7; metro Rambuteau). Bookings advisable. Lunch *menu* 65/95FF.
✉ 40 rue de Gergovie, 14e (2, H7) ☎ 01 45 41 36 88 Ⓜ Pernéty ⏲ Mon-Sat lunch 12-2.15pm, dinner 7-10.30pm **V**

La Cagouille **$$$**
Seafood
Chef Gérard Allemandou, one of the flavours of the 1990s, gets rave reviews for his fish and shellfish dishes at this pleasant cafe-restaurant with its terrace for lunch *al fresco*. Bookings essential. *Menu* 150/250FF.
✉ 10-12 Place Constantin Brancusi, 14e (2, H8) ☎ 01 43 22 09 01 Ⓜ Gaîté ⏲ lunch 12-2.30pm, dinner 7.30-10.30pm

Le Caméléon **$$**
French
Not far from the big names of the blvd Montparnasse, this quaint little place does a nice 'nouveau' bistro turn in a traditional setting. Lobster ravioli is a favourite amongst the loyal habitués, and the Auvergne sausage with *purée maison* is a perfect French rendition of

bangers and mash. Bookings advisable. Lunch menu 120FF.

✉ 6 rue de Chevreuse, 6e (3, K8) ☎ 01 43 20 63 43 Ⓜ Vavin ☉ lunch Mon-Fri 12-2pm, dinner Mon-Sat 8-10.30pm

Monsieur Lapin $$$
French
What's up doc? At least half a dozen different ways of preparing Mr Bunny, that's what. But it's not all rabbit, there's also an impressive range of seafood (eg, warm

oysters in champagne) and other meat dishes – all prepared and served with admirable care and attention. Bookings advisable. *Menu* 185FF.

✉ 11 rue Raymond-Losserand, 14e (2, H8) ☎ 01 43 20 21 39; fax 01 43 21 84 86 Ⓜ Gaîté ☉ lunch Wed-Sun 12-2pm, dinner Tues-Sun 7.30-11pm

La Régalade $$
French
The *plat du jour* of this

unpretentious bistro is the culinary talent of chef Yves Camdeborde. The *menu* might include a salt-cod gazpacho with hot-tomato sorbet or veal kidneys with almonds and a juniper-flavoured sauce. Bookings essential. *Menu* 185FF.

✉ 49 ave Jean-Moulin, 14e (2, J8) ☎ 01 45 45 68 58; fax 01 45 40 96 74 Ⓜ Alésia ☉ lunch Tues-Fri 12-2.30pm, Tues-Sat 7pm-midnight

TROCADÉRO & SOUTH

The 16e is one of the wealthiest and most *huppé* (posh) in Paris. Though there's precious little to do at night, there are a few exceptional (and very classy) restaurants that might tempt you to cross the river.

A&M le bistrot $$
French
The well-respected chefs of Apicius and Marius have joined talents in the bourgeois 16e, and are doing a fine trade in finely tuned modern bistro cuisine. Efficient service and impeccable presentation are what the besuited clientele demand and receive. Bookings advisable. *Menu* 170/205FF.

✉ 136 blvd Murat, 16e (2, G2) ☎ 01 45 27 39 60; fax 01 45 27 69 71 Ⓜ Port de St-Cloud ☉ lunch Mon-Fri 12-2.30pm, dinner Mon-Sat 7.45-10.30pm

La Gare $$
French
The platforms and tracks in this converted railway station have been replaced with an open kitchen and tables, resulting in a spacious, light, welcoming and branché brasserie at the chic end of town. The spe-

ciality of the house is poultry *à la rôtisserie*, perfectly cooked and well presented. Bookings advisable at weekends.

✉ 19 Chausée de la Muette, 16e (2, F4) ☎ 01 42 15 15 31; fax 01 42 15 15 23 Ⓜ La Muette ☉ restaurant:

Coffee Primer
un café – a single shot of espresso
une noisette – a shot of espresso with a spot of milk
un café crème – a shot of espresso lengthened with steamed milk (closest thing to a latte)
un café allongé – an espresso lengthened with hot water (closest thing to American-style coffee)

Simon Bracken

lunch 12-3pm, dinner 7pm-midnight; bar: noon-midnight

Pavillon Panama $$$
French
Just 2 steps from Pont Mirabeau, and with an immense teak terrace-deck for dining right on the banks of the Seine, this spot is popular with the local TV suits and stars, who nibble sandwiches

Food Markets

Paris' food markets – whether temporary or permanent – offer some of the choicest comestibles on the planet, and are an experience not to be missed. They are generally open Tuesday-Saturday 8am-1pm and Sunday 8am-1pm.

Place d'Aligre, 12e; 2, G12; Ⓜ Ledru Rollin; ⊘ mornings only

Blvd de Belleville, 11e; 2, D12; Ⓜ Belleville; ⊘ Tuesday & Friday

Rue de Buci, 6e; 5, A3; Ⓜ Mabillon

Blvd de la Chapelle, 18e; 4, D9; Ⓜ Barbès Rochechouart; ⊘ Wednesday & Saturday

Rue Cler, 7e; 3, F4; Ⓜ École Militaire

Rue Daguerre, 14e; 2, H8; Ⓜ Denfert Rochereau

Rue Montorgueil, 1er; 3, D11; Ⓜ Les Halles

Rue Mouffetard, 5e; 3, K12; Ⓜ Censier Daubenton

Blvd Richard Lenoir, 11e; 3, F15; Ⓜ Bastille; ⊘ Sunday mornings

and tuna grilled with ginger, and while away the hours watching the river flow. Bookings advisable.
✉ **Port de Javel haut, 15e (2, G4)** ☎ 01 44 37 10 21; fax 01 44 37 11 25 ⓔ rene.pou verin@wanadoo.fr Ⓜ Javel ⊘ lunch 12-4pm, dinner 8pm-1am

La Plage Parisienne $$
French
You don't have to worry about sand in your meal at this 'Parisian Beach', under the beautiful Pont Mirabeau. The magnificent wood and glass structures, extended by a renovated barge and an open summer deck, are the perfect place to escape the streets for a light lunch or summer dinner. Bookings advisable. *Menu* 250FF; children's weekend *menu* 100FF.
✉ **Port de Javel haut, 15e (2, G4)** ☎ 01 40 59 41 00 Ⓜ Javel; Mirabeau ⊘ Sun-Fri lunch 12-3pm, Sat dinner 8-11pm ♿ yes

One of Paris' many fresh food markets

Le Totem $$

French

The famous faces at the bar, the spectacular views of the Tour Eiffel and the imaginative and satisfying dishes are just a few of the delights of the très, très branché Totem. Bookings advisable. *Menu 134FF.*

✉ Musée de l'Homme, 17 Place du Trocadéro, 16e (3, E1) ☎ 01 47 27 28 29; fax 01 47 27 53 01 @ restotem@aol.com Ⓜ Trocadéro ◷ noon-2am

MONTMARTRE & PIGALLE

This area encompasses bits of the 9e, 17e and 18e. The restaurants along rue des Trois Frères, 18e (4, D6), are a much better bet than their touristy counterparts around Place du Tertre. Many are open 7 days a week, but only for dinner.

L'Été en Pente Douce $

French

'Summer on a Gentle Slope' neatly sums up this pleasant little cafe with a terrace and charming verandah at the foot of Sacré Cœur. Chef Jean-Luc Brillet serves up carefully prepared dishes such as traditional salads, stuffed capsicums and duck thigh à l'orange. Bookings advisable.

✉ 23 rue Muller, 18e (4, C7) ☎ 01 42 64 02 67; fax 01 46 06 25 67 @ jaeu@wanadoo.fr; www.pariresto.com Ⓜ Barbès Rochechouart; Anvers ◷ Mon-Fri lunch 12-2pm, dinner 8-10pm

La Mascotte $

French

Specialising in seafood and charcuterie, this unassuming little bar/restaurant is an excellent spot to sample oysters, mussels, fish crab and lobster. Bookings advisable. *Menu 63/73/135FF.*

✉ 52 rue des Abbesses, 18e (4, C4) ☎ 01 46 06 28 15; fax 01 42 23 64 06 Ⓜ Abbesses ◷ Tues-Sun 7am-1am

Le Taroudant $$

Moroccan

Discreetly tucked away in the *bon vivant* Abbesses quartier, this traditional Moroccan restaurant satisfies from the genial welcome of the patron to the freshness, lightness and value of its tasty tajines and couscous. Try a drop from the remarkable North African wine list. Bookings advisable.

✉ 8 rue Aristide Bruant, 18e (4, D4) ☎ 01 42 64 95 81 Ⓜ Abbesses; Blanche ◷ Thurs-Tues lunch 11am-3pm, dinner 6.30pm-midnight **V**

INTERNET CAFES

Café Orbital

Paris' premier Internet cafe has 30 high-speed stations (Mac, Windows, Linux) with a full suite of services: ftp, telnet, vid, printers, ethernet jacks etc. Grab a beer and cyberwich and listen to the live grooves while you tap.

✉ 13 rue de Médicis, 6e (5, C3) ☎ 01 43 25 76 77 @ www.cafeorbital.fr Ⓜ Odéon ◷ Mon-Sat 10am-10pm, Sun 12-8pm ⑤ Internet access 55FF/hr, 200/300FF 5/10hrs

Voyageurs du Monde

Innovative travel agency in central Paris with a bookshop, world-food restaurant and a pleasant 14-machine surfing space.

✉ 53 rue Ste-Anne, 2e (3, C9) ☎ 01 42 86 16 00 @ www.vdm.com.fr Ⓜ Pyramides ◷ Mon-Sat 12-7pm ⑤ Internet access 60FF/hr

Web Bar

Sip and surf at the hippest cybercafe in Paris, which also doubles as a gallery, performance space and office-away-from-home for the digitally deprived dealdoers of the Marais.

✉ 32 rue de Picardie, 3e (5, C9) ☎ 01 42 72 66 55 @ www.webbar.fr Ⓜ Filles du Calvaire; Temple ◷ 8.30am-2am ⑤ Internet access 45FF/hr 300FF/10hrs

Going Online

For more information on accessing the Web, see page 116.

entertainment

There's always too much to do in Paris. Whether your musical tastes run to opera, jazz or house, or you prefer theatre, cinema or experimental dance, there's always way too much going on to ever get bored. The French take Culture (with a capital C) seriously, and they match this with invest-

Bill Posters was here

ment in world-class performance spaces, support of creative companies and a general enthusiasm for both classical and fringe arts.

Paris must also rate as one of the best cities in the world for cinema, with around 300 films screening in any particular week, many in English with French subtitles. In addition to first-release English-language and French films, you'll find retrospectives of the great directors (Hitchcock is a perennial favourite) and a sprinkling of films from Africa, Asia and Eastern Europe.

Paris now has 2 great opera houses (Garnier and Bastille) and a rich opera season – though you need to book several months in advance by mail (see the following section for details) to ensure good seats. Tickets range from under 100FF to over 600FF.

The city's music venues are legion, from enormous concert halls to poky (and smoky) little bars and jazz clubs. Keep an ear open for the regular classical music concerts held in many churches.

Bookings & Tickets

Reservations are recommended for all performances. You can buy tickets for many (but not all) cultural events at several ticket outlets, among them **FNAC** (☎ 08 03 02 00 40 or ☎ 08 36 68 04 56 for information in French) outlets and **Virgin Megastore** (☎ 01 49 53 50 00), 52 ave des Champs Élysées, 8e (3, C4). Both make reservations and do ticketing by phone.

Kiosque Théâtre sells half-price tickets (plus 16FF commission) for same-day performances. The 2 agencies, in front of Gare Montparnasse, 15e (3, K7), and opposite 15 Place de la Madeleine, 9e (3, C7), are open Tuesday-Sunday 12-8pm.

Information

It's virtually impossible to sample the richness of Paris' entertainment scene without first perusing *Pariscope* or *L'Officiel des Spectacles*, both of which come out on Wednesday. *Pariscope* includes a 5-page insert in English courtesy of *Time Out* weekly events magazine, and can be found at www.pariscope.fr online. For information on clubs and the music scene, magazines like *Les Inrockuptibles*, *LYLO* and *Nova* are particularly useful.

What's On

January/February *Chinese New Year* – dragon parades and other festivities are held in Chinatown (13e) and rue Au Maire (3e)

March/April *Banlieues Bleues* – this jazz festival held in Saint Denis and other Paris suburbs attracts big-name talent

April *Marathon International de Paris* – mid-month; from Place de la Concorde (1er) to ave Foch (16e)

May/June *Internationaux de France de Tennis* (French Open Tennis Tournament) – held in Stade Roland Garros

June *Gay Pride* – around 20 June; a colourful Saturday-afternoon parade through the Marais to celebrate Gay Pride Day

Fête de la Musique – 21 June; featuring impromptu live performances all over the city

June/July *La Course des Garçons de Café* – hundreds of waiters and waitresses race through central Paris carrying a glass and a bottle balanced on a tray

July *La Goutte d'Or en Fête* – world music festival (raï, reggae, rap etc) at Place de Léon, 18e

Bastille Day – 14 July; on the night of the 13th about a dozen *bals des sapeurs-pompiers* are held at the city's fire stations. At 10am on the 14th, a fire brigade and military parade travels along the Champs Élysées. On the night of the 14th, a huge display of *feux d'artifice* (fireworks) is held at around 11pm either near the Tour Eiffel or at the Invalides.

Street performer

Tour de France – 3rd or 4th Sunday; the world's most prestigious cycling event ends on the Champs Élysées

September *Festival d'Automne* – begins Sept; Autumn Festival of music and theatre held throughout the city over 3 months

October *Foire Internationale d'Art Contemporain (FIAC)* – huge contemporary art fair with some 150 galleries represented at the Espace Eiffel Branly, 29-55 Quai Branly (7e)

December *Christmas Eve Mass* – 24-25 Dec; midnight Mass is celebrated at many Paris churches, including Notre Dame

New Year's Eve – 31 Dec; festivities take place on blvd St-Michel (5e), Place de la Bastille (11e) and the Champs Élysées (8e)

THEATRE & COMEDY

Almost all of Paris' theatre productions are performed in French. There are a few English-speaking troupes around, though – look for ads on metro poster boards and in English-language periodicals (eg *FUSAC* – France USA Contacts).

Les Abbesses (4, D5)
The new neoclassical home for the Théâtre de la Ville is the venue for mainly contemporary theatre, music and dance works.
✉ **31 rue des Abbesses, 18e**
☎ **01 42 74 22 77**
Ⓜ **Abbesses** ⏱ box office Tues-Sat 5-8pm; by ☎ Mon-Sat 11am-7pm ⑤ 95-190FF

Bouffes du Nord
(2, C11) Best known as the Paris base of Peter Brooks' experimental theatre troupe, this theatre also hosts works by other directors (notably Stéphane Lissner), as well as classical and jazz concerts.
✉ **37bis blvd de la Chapelle, 10e** ☎ **01 46 07 34 50** Ⓜ **La Chapelle** ⏱ Tues-Sat 8.30pm, Sat 4pm; box office Mon-Sat 11am-6pm ⑤ 70-130FF; matinees 50-110FF

Café de la Gare
One of the best and most innovative cafe-theatres in Paris, with acts ranging from reinterpreted classics to comic theatre and stand-up.
✉ **41 rue du Temple, 4e (5, C7)**
☎ **01 42 78 52 51**
ⓔ **perso.club.intern et.fr/blix/cdlg.htm**
Ⓜ **Hôtel de Ville; Rambuteau** ⏱ Wed-Sat 8 & 10pm ⑤ 100-120/50-100FF

Comédie Française
(3, D9) The world's oldest national theatre (founded in 1680 under Louis XIV), with a repertoire based on the works of French luminaries such as Corneille, Molière, Racine, Beaumarchais, Marivaux and Musset. In recent years contemporary and even non-French works have been staged in its 3 theatres.
✉ **2 rue de Richelieu, 1er** ☎ **01 40 15 00 15**; box office ☎ **01 44 58 15 15** ⓔ **www.come die-francaise.fr**
Ⓜ **Palais Royal** ⏱ box office 11am-6pm daily ⑤ 70-190FF; discounts for over 60s and students

Laughing Matters
The best place in town for English-language belly laughs, hosting a regular stream of stand-ups from across the Channel, or drying out on the way back home from Edinburgh.
✉ **Hôtel du Nord, 102 Quai de Jemmapes, 10e (3, B14)** ☎ **01 48 06 01 20** Ⓜ **République** ⏱ Sun-Tues 8.30pm ⑤ 100/80FF

Odéon Théâtre de l'Europe (5, B3)
This huge, ornate theatre, built in the early 1780s, stages great French classics as well as contemporary plays and works in their original languages (sub-titled in French). It also often hosts theatre troupes from abroad.
✉ **1 Place Paul Claudel, 6e** ☎ **01 44 41 36 00**; box office ☎ **01 44 41 36 36**
ⓔ **www.theatre-od eon.fr** Ⓜ **Odéon** ⏱ box office 11am-7pm ⑤ 30-180FF; discounted tickets available 90mins before curtain; discounts for over 60s and students

Point Virgule (3, F13)
This popular spot in the Marais offers cafe-theatre at its best, with stand-up comics, performance artists, musical acts – you name it. The quality is variable, but it's great fun nevertheless.
✉ **7 rue Ste-Croix de la Bretonnerie, 4e**
☎ **01 42 78 67 03**
Ⓜ **Hôtel de Ville** ⏱ 8, 9.15 & 10.15pm ⑤ 80/130/150FF for 1/2/3 shows, students 65FF for 1 show (not Sat)

Théâtre de la Bastille
Probably the best fringe theatre venue in town, with a variety of experimental works including text, movement and music.
✉ **76 rue de la Roquette, 11e (2, F12)**
☎ **01 43 57 42 14**
Ⓜ **Bastille; Voltaire** ⏱ box office Mon-Fri 10am-1pm & 2-6.30pm, Sat-Sun 2-6.30pm ⑤ 120/80FF plus discounts for seniors & students

CLASSICAL MUSIC, OPERA & DANCE

Centre Mandapa
(2, J10) Theatre dedicated to traditional and contemporary ethnic dance and theatre, with a particular emphasis on India (such as the Kutiyattam dance theatre of Kerala).
✉ 6 rue Wurtz, 13e
☎ 01 45 89 01 60
@ ourworld.com
puserve.com/home
pages/MANDAPA/
Ⓜ Glacière Ⓢ 80-
100/60-70FF

Cité de la Musique
(2, B13) The 1200-seat main auditorium hosts every imaginable type of music and dance. Students at the Conservatoire National Supérieur de Musique et de Danse
(☎ 01 40 40 45 45) perform free orchestral concerts and recitals several times a week.
✉ 221 ave Jean
Jaurès, 19e ☎ 01 44
84 45 45/☎ 01 44 84
44 84 @ www.cite-mus
ique.fr Ⓜ Porte de
Pantin ⏰ box office
Tues-Sun 12-6pm
Ⓢ 75-200FF, discounts
for seniors & students

Opéra Bastille
(3, G15) The Opéra National de Paris splits its performances between here and the Opéra Garnier, its old home. The Opéra Bastille opened in 1989 and, like the Opéra Garnier, it also stages ballets and concerts put on by the Opéra National's affiliated orchestra, choir and ballet companies. The opera season lasts from mid-September to mid-July.
✉ 2-6 Place de la
Bastille, 12e ☎ 01 44

Opéra Garnier

73 13 99/☎ 08 36 69
78 68; reservations
☎ 08 36 69 78 68
@ www.opera-de-pa
ris.fr Ⓜ Bastille
⏰ box office Mon-Sat
11am-6.30pm Ⓢ 60-
670FF opera, 50-420FF
ballet, 45-255FF concerts; unsold tickets sold to students, under 25s and over 65s for about 100FF 15mins before curtain. Book by mail (120 rue de Lyon, 75576 Paris Cedex 12) 10 weeks in advance or by phone 4 weeks prior

Opéra Comique
A century-old hall that plays host to classic and

lesser-known works of opera. The season lasts from late October to early July.
✉ 5 rue Favart, 2e (3,
B10) ☎ 01 42 44 45 46
Ⓜ Richelieu Drouot
⏰ box office (opp 14
rue Favart) Mon-Sat
11am-7pm Ⓢ 100-
610FF; 50FF tickets with limited or no visibility up to 12hrs before curtain; discounts 15mins before curtain for students, youth and seniors

Opéra Garnier (3, B9)
The extravagant Opéra Garnier is the traditional home of the Opéra

Opéra Bastille

National de Paris, which now splits its performances between here and the Opéra Bastille. While most of the major opera performances are held at Bastille, the Opéra Garnier offers a much more special experience with outstanding acoustics, though not all seats have great views.

✉ Place de l'Opéra, 9e
☎ 01 44 73 13 99/
☎ 08 36 69 78 68;
reservations ☎ 08 36 69 78 68 @ www
.opera-de-paris.fr
Ⓜ Opéra ⏱ box office Mon-Sat 11am-6.30pm.
Ⓢ 60-670FF opera, 30-280FF ballet; unsold tickets sold to students, under 25s and over 65s for about 100FF 15mins before curtain. Tickets go on sale 2 weeks prior to the performance; book by mail (120 rue de Lyon, 75576 Paris Cedex 12) 10 weeks in advance to ensure your reservation or by phone 4 weeks prior

Regard du Cygne

Many of Paris' young and daring talents in movement, music and theatre congregate around this interesting performance space in Belleville. If you're in the mood for some innovative modern dance – performance or participation – this is the place.

✉ 210 rue de Belleville, 20e (2, D13)
☎ 01 43 58 55 93
Ⓜ Place des Fêtes
Ⓢ 70FF; discounts for students, seniors and unemployed or 30mins prior to curtain

Salle Pleyel (3, A3)

A highly regarded, 1920s-era hall that hosts many of Paris' finest classical music concerts and recitals.

✉ 252 rue du Faubourg St-Honoré, 8e
☎ 01 45 61 53 00
Ⓜ Ternes ⏱ box office Mon-Sat 11am-6pm
Ⓢ 80-410FF

Théâtre des Champs Élysées (3, D4)

A prestigious Right Bank orchestral and recital hall, infamous as the venue where Stravinsky debuted his controversial *Le Sacre du Printemps* in 1913. Popular Sunday concerts are held year-round at 11am.

✉ 15 ave Montaigne, 8e ☎ 01 49 52 50 50
Ⓜ Alma-Marceau
⏱ box office Mon-Sat 11am-7pm Ⓢ 50-700FF

Théâtre Musical de Paris (5, B6)

Also called the Théâtre Municipal du Châtelet or just the Théâtre du Châtelet, this hall was recently reopened after a year-long renovation. It hosts operas, concerts (including some by the excellent Orchestre de Paris) and theatre performances.

✉ 1 Place du Châtelet, 1er ☎ 01 42 33 00 00; reservations ☎ 01 40 28 28 40 @ www.the atre-chatelet.com
Ⓜ Châtelet ⏱ box office Mon-Sat 10am-7pm Ⓢ 50-750FF opera, 90-200FF ballet, Sun concerts 120/60FF; students, under 25s and over 65s 50FF 15mins before curtain (not opera)

Auditorium ceiling by Marc Chagall, Opéra Garnier

Simon Bracken

ROCK, JAZZ & FRENCH CHANSONS

Paris has been an important jazz centre since the 1920s, and the city's better *boîtes* (clubs) continue to attract top international stars. The Banlieues Bleues, a jazz festival held in Saint Denis and other Paris suburbs, also attracts big-name talent.

There's rock at numerous bars, cafes and clubs around. Typically, tickets cost 120-250FF. The most popular stadium venues for international acts include Le Zénith (☎ 01 42 08 60 00) at the Cité de la Musique in the 19e and the Palais Omnisports de Paris-Bercy (☎ 01 44 68 44 68), 12e.

Au Duc des Lombards
This ultra-cool venue, decorated with posters of past jazz greats, attracts a far more relaxed (and less reverent) crowd than the other 2 venues on the same street.
⊠ 42 rue des Lombards, 1er (5, B6)
☎ 01 42 33 22 88
Ⓜ Châtelet ☺ 8pm-4am Ⓢ 80-100FF

Au Vieux Paris
A real period-piece Parisian bar which hosts sing-alongs of French *chansons* (sheet music provided), accompanied by an accordionist and Madame Françoise, the feisty proprietor. The patrons are mostly young Parisians. Arrive around 11pm to get a seat.
⊠ 72 rue de la Verrerie, 4e (5, C7)
☎ 01 48 87 55 56
Ⓜ Hôtel de Ville
☺ Thurs-Sat 11.45pm

Le Baiser Salé
One of 3 very hip jazz clubs on the same street at which a single membership card (150FF a year) gets you significant discounts. The *salle de jazz* on the 1st floor has concerts of Afro jazz, jazz fusion etc. There's a bar on the ground floor.

⊠ 58 rue des Lombards, 1er (5, B6)
☎ 01 42 33 37 71
Ⓜ Châtelet ☺ bar 7pm-6am; *salle de jazz* 10pm-3am Ⓢ 60-100FF; Sun-Mon free

Le Bataclan
Popular mid-sized venue featuring an eclectic mix of international rock, French bands, world music and even French chanson.
⊠ 50 blvd Voltaire, 11e (5, C10) ☎ 01 47 00 55 22 Ⓜ Oberkampf ☺ 8pm-late Ⓢ 100-200FF

Le Caveau de la Huchette
A medieval *caveau* (cellar) – used as a torture chamber during the Revolution – where virtually all the jazz greats have played since 1946. It's touristy, but the atmosphere can often be more electric than at the more 'serious' jazz clubs. Details on coming attractions are posted on the door.
⊠ 5 rue de la Huchette, 5e (5, C4)
☎ 01 43 26 65 05
Ⓜ St-Michel
☺ 9.30pm-2.30am (Fri to 3.30am, Sat to 4am)
Ⓢ Mon-Thurs 60FF (55FF students); Fri-Sat 70FF (no discounts)

Chez Louisette
This is one of the highlights of a visit to Paris' largest flea market. Market-goers crowd around little tables to eat lunch and hear an old-time *chanteuse* belt out Edith Piaf numbers accompanied by accordion music.
⊠ Marché aux Puces de St-Ouen, inside the maze of Marché Vernaison not far from 130 ave Michelet (2, A9) ☎ 01 40 12 10 14 Ⓜ Porte de Clignancourt ☺ Sat-Mon 12-7pm

La Cigale (4, E6)
This converted theatre has been a favourite of visiting rock, punk and indie bands for years. It's also a fave of audiences with its huge capacity, faded good looks and bouncy mosh pit.
⊠ 102 blvd Rochechouart, 18e
☎ 01 49 25 89 99
Ⓜ Pigalle ☺ 8.30pm
Ⓢ 12-160FF

Le Divan du Monde
(4, E5) One of the best concert venues in town with good visibility and sound; Latino figures at least once a week. It's also a popular club, open most nights till dawn.
⊠ 75 rue des Martyrs

☎ 01 44 92 77 66
Ⓜ Pigalle ◷ Mon-Sat
7.30pm, Sun 4pm
Ⓢ Tues-Sat 60-110FF,
Mon free

Le Lapin Agile (4, B5)

A rustic cabaret venue
favoured by turn-of-the-
century artists and intellectuals. The name derives
from *Le Lapin à Gill*, a
mural of a rabbit jumping
out of a cooking pot by
caricaturist André Gill,
which can still be seen on
the western exterior wall.
These days, chansons are
performed and poetry read
nightly.

✉ 22 rue des Saules,
18e ☎ 01 46 06 85 87
Ⓜ Lamarck Caulaincourt
◷ Tues-Sun 9pm-2am
Ⓢ 130/90FF

Théâtre du Tourtour

This is an intimate, 123-
seat theatre housed in a
15th-century cellar. The
entertainment includes
plays by young theatre
companies at 7pm; classi-
cal or modern plays by
more experienced actors at
8.30pm; music – anything
from rock to French chan-
sons – at 10.15pm.

✉ 20 rue Quincampoix,
4e (5, B7) ☎ 01 48 87

82 48 Ⓜ Châtelet
◷ Tues-Sat 10pm
Ⓢ 70-100/20FF

La Villa

This very cool, high-tech
place attracts big-name
performers from around
the world, with local talent
thrown in for good meas-
ure between sets. You'll
love the unusual furnish-
ings – stools shaped like
teardrops, 'crouching'
chairs etc.

✉ 29 rue Jacob, 6e (3,
F9) ☎ 01 43 26 60 00
Ⓜ St-Germain des Prés
◷ Mon-Sat 10.30pm-
2am Ⓢ 120-150FF

DANCE CLUBS

Les Bains

Located in a renovated old
Turkish bathhouse, this
club still manages to
produce steam heat on
particularly hot nights.
Once renowned for its
surly, selective bouncers on
the outside and trendy,
star-struck revellers inside,
Les Bains has calmed
down a bit under new
management, but it's still

tough to crack on the
weekend. Monday is
theme night. Mostly
techno with a healthy dash
of 70s disco, it attracts a
mixed straight and gay
crowd.

✉ 7 rue du Bourg
l'Abbé, 3e (3, D12)
☎ 01 48 87 01 80
Ⓜ Étienne Marcel
◷ 11.30pm-6.30am
Ⓢ 100FF

Le Balajo

A mainstay of the Parisian
dance-hall scene since
1936. Wednesday is
mambo night; Thursday-
Saturday the DJs spin rock,
1970s disco, funk etc. On
Sunday afternoon, DJs play
old-fashioned *musette*
(accordion music) – waltz,
tango, cha-cha – for afi-
cionados of *rétro* tea dancing. Jacket required.

✉ 9 rue de Lappe, 11e
(2, F12) ☎ 01 47 00 07
87 Ⓜ Bastille
◷ 11.30pm-5.30am,
Sun 3-7pm Ⓢ 100FF
(80FF Wed, 40FF
women; 50FF Sun)

La Chapelle des Lombards

Something of a pick-up
place, where Antillean,
African and Latin American
beats create a very lively
dance scene. There's usually a live concert Thursday
at 8pm (70FF). Punters
wearing trainers (sneakers)
won't get in.

✉ 19 rue de Lappe,

Boîtes

A *boîte* (literally 'box') is just about any sort of place
where music leads to dancing. The truly *branché*
(trendy) crowd considers showing up before 1am a
serious breach of good taste.

The boîtes favoured by the Parisian 'in' crowd
change frequently, and many are officially private.
Single men may not be admitted, even if their
clothes are subculturally appropriate, simply because
they're single men. Women, on the other hand, get
in for free on some nights. It's always easier to get
into the club of your choice during the week – when
things may be hopping even more than they are at
the weekend. Parisians tend to go out in groups and
may not mingle as much as you're used to.

11e (2, F12) ☎ 01 43 57 24 24 Ⓜ Bastille ⏰ Tues-Sat 10.30pm-5am (Sat-Sun to 6am) ⑤ 100FF (120FF Fri-Sat); free for women before midnight

Club Zed
An arched stone basement where the DJs favour rock-'n'roll, jazz and swing.
⊠ 2 rue des Anglais, 5e (5, C4) ☎ 01 43 54 93 78 Ⓜ Maubert Mutualité ⏰ Wed-Sat 10.30pm-3am (Fri-Sat to 5am) ⑤ 50FF (100FF Fri-Sat)

Ekivök
A new kid in town that dares to bill itself as 'la disco libertine du Marais' (literally, the licentious disco of the Marais) must have something going for it. There's a tea dance on Thursday from 3-8pm.
⊠ 40 rue des Blancs Manteaux, 4e (5, C7) ☎ 01 42 71 71 41 Ⓜ Rambuteau ⏰ 11pm-6am

Le Gibus
This former rock mecca (Police, the Clash) still drags in the crowds. While it has added house and trance to the mix, it's still doing the business.
⊠ 18 rue du Faubourg-du-Temple, 11e (3, C15) ☎ 01 47 00 78 88 Ⓜ République ⏰ Wed-Sun midnight-dawn ⑤ Wed-Thurs free, Fri-Sun 100FF

La Guinguette Pirate
This club, situated on a 3-masted Chinese junk on the Seine at the foot of the Bibliothèque National de France, is as eclectic as it gets: from reggae and ska to Breton rock. There's usually a concert at 10.30pm;

the crowd is young (25 to 30) and energetic. Weekend concerts (9pm) feature French rock groups.
⊠ 157 Quai de la Gare, 13e (2, H12) ☎ 01 56 29 10 20 Ⓜ Quai de la Gare ⏰ noon-2.30am (Mon from 7.30pm) ⑤ 30FF for concerts

La Java
The original dance hall where Piaf got her first break now reverberates to the sound of salsa at the 'Cuban Jam Sessions', featuring live and recorded sounds and some hot dancing.
⊠ 105 rue du Faubourg-du-Temple, 10e (2, D12) ☎ 01 42 02 20 52 Ⓜ Belleville ⏰ Thurs-Fri 11pm-6am ⑤ 60-100FF

La Locomotive
An enormous, ever-popular disco that's long been one of the favourite dancing venues for teenage out-of-towners. Music at La Loco ranges from techno in the pulsating basement to groove and disco in the 1st-floor loft; psychedelic, rock and the like dominate on the huge ground floor. There's a popular gay tea dance here on Sunday from 5-11pm.

⊠ 90 blvd de Clichy, 18e (4, D3) ☎ 01 53 41 88 88 Ⓜ Blanche ⏰ 11pm-6am (Sat-Sun to 7am, Mon from midnight) ⑤ 60FF Fri-Sat before midnight (100FF after); 55FF Mon-Fri, women free before 12.30am; Sun men 70FF & women free

Rex Club
This huge, popular club is the undisputed king (for now) of techno and house; features music and video DJs.
⊠ 5 blvd Poissonière, 2e (3, C11) ☎ 01 42 36 83 98 Ⓜ Bonne Nouvelle ⏰ Tues-Sat 11pm-dawn ⑤ 60-80FF

Slow Club
An unpretentious disco housed in a deep cellar once used to ripen Caribbean bananas. The live bands attract students as well as older couples. The music varies from night to night but includes jazz, boogie, bebop, swing and blues.
⊠ 130 rue de Rivoli, 1er (5, A6) ☎ 01 42 33 84 30 Ⓜ Châtelet ⏰ Tues-Sat 10pm-3am (Fri-Sat to 4am) ⑤ 60FF (75FF Fri-Sat); students small discount

Dockside dance club

CINEMAS

Pariscope and *L'Officiel des Spectacles* list the cinematic offerings alphabetically by their French title followed by the English (or German, Italian, Spanish etc) one. If a movie is labelled 'vo' (for *version originale*) it means it will be subtitled rather than dubbed ('vf or *version française*), so 'vo' Hollywood movies will still be in English.

Le Champo

One of the most popular of the many Quartier Latin cinemas, featuring classics and retrospectives along the lines of Hitchcock, Jacques Tati, Frank Capra and Woody Allen.
✉ 51 rue des Écoles, 5e (5, C3) ☎ 43 54 51 60 Ⓜ St-Michel; Cluny La Sorbonne Ⓢ 43/33FF; matinee 27FF

Cinéma des Cinéastes

Founded by the 3 Claudes (Miller, Berri and Lelouch) and *Betty Blue* director Jean-Jacques Beneix, this 3-screen cinema is dedicated to quality cinema, whether French, foreign or avant-garde. Thematic seasons, documentaries and meet-the-director sessions round out the program.
✉ 7 ave de Clichy (4, D1) ☎ 01 53 42 40 20 Ⓜ Place de Clichy Ⓢ 43/35FF

Cinémathèque Française (3, D2)

This government-supported cultural institution almost always leaves its foreign

Le Champo

offerings – often seldom-screened classics – in the original, nondubbed version. There are 2 cinemas, 1 at the Palais de Chaillot, the other at 42 blvd Bonne Nouvelle, 10e (metro Bonne Nouvelle).
✉ Palais de Chaillot, 7 ave Albert de Mun, 16e ☎ 01 53 65 74 74; recorded program ☎ 01 56 26 01 01 🖳 www.cinematheque.tm. fr Ⓜ Trocadéro; Iéna ⏰ Tues-Sun Ⓢ 29/18FF

Grand Action

The flagship cinema of the Action chain, which specialises in grand cinema events in both English and French – often new prints of classics such as Kubrick's *Spartacus*. Retrospectives include gems from the Golden Years of Hollywood or more recent classics such as the films of Jim Jarmusch.
✉ 5 rue des Écoles, 5e (5, E4) ☎ 01 43 29 44 40 Ⓜ Cardinal Lemoine Ⓢ 40/32/25FF

Le Studio des Ursulines

Legendary art-house cinema nowadays adopting a more eclectic program of first-release avant-garde pieces, retrospectives, lost classics and more popular movies.
✉ 10 rue des Ursulines, 5e (3, J10) ☎ 01 43 26 19 09 🚉 RER Luxembourg Ⓢ 40/32FF

UGC Ciné Cité Les Halles

The enormous 16-screen cinema complex in the underground Les Halles shopping mall screens mainly first-run features, including Hollywood blockbusters. The seats are among the most comfortable in town, and some of the screens are so wide you need to turn your head tennis-match style to follow an onscreen conversation.
✉ Forum des Halles, 1er (5, A7) ☎ 08 36 68 68 58 Ⓜ Châtelet Les Halles

Going to the Movies

Going to the movies in Paris does not come cheaply: expect to pay around 50FF for a ticket. Students and people under 18 and over 60 usually get discounts of about 25% except on Friday, Saturday and Sunday nights. On Wednesday (and sometimes Monday) most cinemas give discounts to everyone.

PUBS, BARS & CAFES

L'Armagnac

A bustling lunch spot by day, by night the Armagnac has just the right levels of smoke, noise and local flavour to give it the authenticity that more self-conscious bars closer to Bastille struggle to replicate.

✉ 104 rue de Charonne, 11e (2, F13) ☎ 01 43 71 49 43 Ⓜ Charonne ◷ Mon-Fri 7am-2am, Sat-Sun 10.30am-2am

L'Autre Café

This new venture by the owners of Le Troisième Bureau has already begun to move the centre of after-dark activity west of rue Oberkampf. With its long bar, open spaces, relaxed environment and reasonable prices, it attracts a mixed young crowd of locals, artists and party-goers.

✉ 62 rue Jean-Pierre Timbaud, 11e (2, E12) ☎ 01 40 21 03 07 Ⓜ Parmentier ◷ 9am-2am

Buddha Bar

At centre stage in the cavernous cellar of this restaurant/bar frequented by suits, supermodels and hangers-on is an enormous bronze Buddha. Everyone should go at least once for a look, but stick with the drinks (cocktails from 60FF); a Pacific Rim-style meal will cost you upwards of 300FF.

✉ 8 rue Boissy d'Anglas, 8e (3, C7) ☎ 01 53 05 90 00 Ⓜ Concorde ◷ 6pm-2am

Café Noir

It may be a bit out of the way, being on the edge of the Sentier garments district, but this funky cafe/bar draws a crowd of Anglo and Francophones well into the night, attracted by the friendly ambience and reasonable prices.

✉ 65 rue Montmartre, 2e (3, C11) ☎ 01 40 39 07 36 Ⓜ Sentier ◷ Mon-Fri 8am-2am, Sat 4pm-2am

Café Oz

A casual, friendly Australian pub with Foster's on tap, plus Australian wines by the glass. The Aussie staff are clued in about jobs, apartments etc. There's a second Café Oz (☎ 01 40 39 00 18) across the river at 18 rue St-Denis, 1er (5, B6).

✉ 184 rue St-Jacques, 5e (5, D3) ☎ 01 43 54 30 48 🚇 RER Luxembourg ◷ 4pm-2am (happy hour to 9.30pm)

China Club

This stylish establishment has a restaurant and huge bar with high ceilings on the ground floor, a *fumoir* on the 1st floor and a jazz club in the cellar – all done up to look like Shanghai circa 1930. Happy hour is 7-9pm daily when all drinks (including the excellent martinis) are 35FF. If you like the style of the China Club, check out its sister bar/restaurant, Le Fumoir, at 6 rue de l'Amiral de Coligny, 1er (5, A5).

✉ 50 rue de Charenton, 12e (2, G12) ☎ 01 43 43 82 02 Ⓜ Ledru Rollin ◷ 7pm-2am

La Closerie des Lilas

Anyone who's ever read Hemingway knows he did a lot of writing, drinking and eating of oysters at this classy bar, and little brass tags on the tables tell you exactly where he (and other luminaries such as Picasso, Apollinaire etc) whiled away the hours being creative or just gossiping. Great summer terrace.

✉ 171 blvd du Montparnasse, 6e (3, K9) ☎ 01 40 51 34 50 Ⓜ Port Royal ◷ 11.30am-1am

Le Clown Bar

This wonderful wine bar next to the Cirque d'Hiver is like a museum with painted ceilings, mosaics and a lovely round bar. The food is simple and unpretentious.

✉ 114 rue Amelot, 11e (5, D10) ☎ 01 43 55 87 35 Ⓜ Filles du Calvaire ◷ Mon-Sat 12-3pm & 7.30pm-1am, Sun 7pm-1am

Martin Moos

Spot the Aussie at Café Oz

Les Étages

Head upstairs to the 2 upper floors for grunge, with graffiti on the walls and big leather armchairs. The drinks aren't cheap (55FF-60FF for spirits), but you do get to phone through your order on an ancient 1950s telephone. Happy hour is 5-9pm.
✉ **35 rue Vieille du Temple, 4e (5, D7)**
☎ **01 42 78 72 00**
Ⓜ **Hôtel de Ville**
◷ Mon-Fri 11am-2am, Sat-Sun 11am-2am

La Flèche d'Or Café

This bar – in a disused train station south-east of Père Lachaise Cemetery – attracts a trendy and arty (not to forget grungy) young crowd; this may as well be Berlin. The big cafe here does a decent brunch on Sunday.
✉ **102bis rue de Bagnolet, 20e (2, E14)**
☎ **01 43 72 04 23**
Ⓜ **Porte de Bagnolet**
◷ 10am-2am

Harry's Bar

One of the most popular pre-war American bars (habitués included Ernest Hemingway and Scott Fitzgerald), this place still makes the best martini in Paris. The Cuban mahogany bar was imported from Manhattan's 3rd Ave in 1911.
✉ **5 rue Daunou, 2e (3, C9)** ☎ **01 42 61 71 14**
Ⓜ **Opéra** ◷ Mon-Sat 10.30am-4am

Le Mecano Bar

Housed in a former tool shed, the ultra-cool Mecano is a good place to meet before heading elsewhere around rue Oberkampf to eat and party.
✉ **99 rue Oberkampf, 11e (2, E12)** ☎ **01 40 21 35 28** Ⓜ **Parmentier**
◷ 8pm-2am

La Perla

A favourite with younger Parisians, this trendy California-style Mexican bar serves up guacamole, nachos and burritos. Happy hour (cocktails, tequila and mezcal only) 6-8pm Monday to Friday.
✉ **26 rue François Miron, 4e (5, D7)** ☎ **01 42 77 59 40** Ⓜ **St-Paul;** **Hôtel de Ville** ◷ Mon-Fri 12-3pm & 7-11pm, Sat-Sun 12-11pm

Le Pick Clops

In a very gay neighbourhood, this straight, down-market rock bar with cheap drinks is a great place to watch the world go by. The brief happy hour is 8-9pm.
✉ **16 rue Vieille du Temple, 4e (5, D7)**
☎ **01 40 29 02 18**
Ⓜ **Hôtel de Ville**
◷ Mon-Sat 8am-2am, Sun 2pm-midnight

Piment Café

This small and cosmopolitan bar changes face frequently, with tranquil moments punctuated by live music, art on show and good, reasonably priced food.
✉ **15 rue de Sévigné, 4e (5, D8)** ☎ **01 42 74 33 75** Ⓜ **St-Paul**
◷ noon-1am (Sun from 6pm)

SanzSans

By night this full-on watering hole is one of the liveliest (OK, rowdiest) drinking spots on the Bastille beat: dress (or undress) to impress. By day the red velvet decor seems a mite overdone.
✉ **49 rue du Faubourg St-Antoine, 11e (2, F12)**
☎ **01 44 75 78 78**
Ⓜ **Bastille** ◷ 9am-2am

Le Troisième Bureau

A pub-cum-*bistrot* with an interesting clientele where you can read, listen to music and even send or receive a fax.
✉ **74 rue de la Folie Méricourt, 11e (3, D15)**
☎ **01 43 55 87 65**
Ⓜ **Oberkampf**
◷ 11.30am-2am (Sun from 6.30pm)

Le Viaduc Café

The terrace of this very trendy cafe in one of the glassed-in arches of the Viaduc des Arts is an excellent spot to while away the hours, and the jazz brunch on Sunday is very popular.
✉ **43 ave Daumesnil, 12e (2, G12)** ☎ **01 44 74 70 70** Ⓜ **Gare de Lyon** ◷ 9am-4am

La Flèche d'Or Café

Simon Bracken

GAY & LESBIAN PARIS

The Marais – especially the areas around the intersection of rue des Archives and rue Ste-Croix de la Bretonnerie (4e), and eastward to rue Vieille du Temple – has been Paris' main centre of gay social life since the early 1980s. There are also some decent bars west of blvd de Sébastopol in the 1er and 2e.

L'Arène
For those seriously OFB (out for business), this place can oblige. It's got dark rooms and cubicles on 3 levels and heats up (boils over, rather) from around midnight. Take the usual precautions.
✉ 80 Quai de l'Hôtel de Ville, 4e (5, C6)
Ⓜ Hôtel de Ville
🕐 2pm-6am (7am weekend)

Banana Café
This ever-popular male cruise bar on 2 levels has an enclosed terrace with stand-up tables and attracts a young crowd. Happy hour is 4.30-7.30pm.
✉ 13 rue de la Ferronnerie, 1er (5, B6)
☎ 01 42 33 35 31
Ⓜ Châtelet Les Halles
🕐 4.15pm-6am

Café Cox
OK, it's got an in-your-face name but this small bar attracts an interesting, rather friendly crowd.
✉ 15 rue des Archives, 4e (5, C7) ☎ 01 42 72 08 00 Ⓜ Hôtel de Ville
🕐 1pm-2am

La Champmeslé
A relaxed, dimly lit place that plays mellow music for its patrons, about 75% of whom are lesbians (the rest are mostly gay men). The back room is reserved for women only. Traditional French chansons are per-formed live every Thursday at 10pm.
✉ 4 rue Chabanais, 2e (3, C9) ☎ 01 42 96 85 20 Ⓜ Pyramides
🕐 Mon-Sat 5pm-2am

Duplex Bar
One of the oldest gay bars in Paris (in every sense), the dark, avant-garde Duplex doubles as some-thing of a gallery with art shows every month.
✉ 25 rue Michel Le Comte, 3e (5, B8)
☎ 01 42 72 80 86
Ⓜ Rambuteau 🕐 8pm-2am

Open Café
This is the place people head for after work to start off the evening. It gets so packed that the clientele spills out onto the pave-ment. Happy hour is 6-8pm.
✉ 17 rue des Archives, 4e (5, C7) ☎ 01 42 72 26 18 Ⓜ Hôtel de Ville
🕐 10am-2am

Le Queen
The best spot in town for all-night drag party action. Boys only Thursday and Disco Inferno Monday.
✉ 102 ave des Champs Élysées, 8e (3, B4) ☎ 01 53 89 08 90 Ⓜ George V
🕐 11pm-dawn Ⓢ free Mon-Fri; Sat-Sun 100FF

Quetzal Bar
A neon-lit, ultramodern bar popular with gay 30-some-thing men. Happy hours 5-8pm and 11pm-midnight.
✉ 10 rue de la Verrerie, 4e (5, C7)
☎ 01 48 87 99 07 Ⓜ Hôtel de Ville 🕐 5pm-3am (Fri-Sat to 4am)

Les Scandaleuses
Glossy and lively lesbian bar in the Marais, popular with artists and designers. Women only.
✉ 8 rue des Ecouffes, 4e (5, D7) ☎ 01 48 87 39 26 Ⓜ Hôtel de Ville
🕐 6pm-2am

Simon Bracken

Apéritifs
Early evening is *apéritif* time in cafes throughout Paris. The most popular tipples are wine (*rouge* or *blanc*); beer (*une pression* is a draught beer); *pastis*, an aniseed-flavoured drink mixed with water to taste; and *kir*, an extract of black-berries normally mixed with white wine, or with cham-pagne to make a *kir royal*.

SPECTATOR SPORTS

For details on upcoming sporting events, consult the sports daily *L'Équipe*, or *Figaroscope* published by *Le Figaro* each Wednesday.

Cycling

Since 1974 the final stage of the Tour de France, the world's most prestigious cycling event, has concluded on the Champs Élysées. The final day varies from year to year but is usually the 3rd or 4th Sunday in July, sometime between 12 and 6pm. The frenetic pace of track cycling comes to the **Palais Omnisports de Paris-Bercy** (2, H12; ☎ 01 44 68 44 68) in winter with the Grand Prix des Nations (October) and the Paris 6-day (January).

Football

Le foot (soccer) has gained even more popularity since France won the World Cup at home in 1998, and Paris hosts its fair share of international events. Paris-Saint Germain football team plays its home games at the **Parc des Princes** (2, G2). The 80,000-seat **Stade de France** (☎ 01 55 93 00 00) in Saint Denis hosted the World Cup finals, and is the major venue for soccer and rugby alike.

Horse Racing

If fillies are your thing, there are 6 racecourses around Paris for you to lose your shirt. Show jumping is all the rage in Paris and the Jumping International de Paris, held in March at the **Palais Omnisports de Paris-Bercy** (2, H12; ☎ 01 44 68 44 68), attracts thousands of fans.

Rugby

Rugby is a popular sport in France and the local club is Le Racing Club de France, whose home ground is **Stade Yves du Manoir** (☎ 01 45 67 55 86) in Colombe.

Tour de France

Tennis

In late May/early June the tennis world focuses on the clay surface of **Stade Roland Garros** (☎ 01 47 43 48 00) in the Bois de Boulogne (2, G2) for the second of the four Grand Slam tournaments. The Paris Indoor tournament is held in late October/early November at the **Palais Omnisports de Paris-Bercy** (2, H12; ☎ 01 44 68 44 68).

MAJOR VENUES

Hippodrome d'Auteuil (2, F3)

One of the cheapest ways to spend a relaxing afternoon in the company of Parisians of all ages and walks of life is to go to the races. The Hippodrome d'Auteuil is the most accessible of Paris' 6 racecourses, and hosts steeplechases from February to early July and early September to early December. The minimum bet is only 10FF. *Paris Turf* publishes a program. ✉ Bois de Boulogne, 16e ☎ 01 45 27 12 25/☎ 01 49 10 20 30 Ⓜ Porte d'Auteuil ⊘ Sun 2pm Ⓢ free to stand on the *pelouse* (lawn); a seat in the *tribune* (stands) 25FF

(40FF Sun and holidays, 50FF special events)

Palais Omnisports de Paris-Bercy (2, H12)

This enormous sports complex on the edge of the city hosts events ranging from gymnastics to ice hockey and ballroom dancing to sumo. ✉ 8 blvd de Bercy, 12e ☎ 01 40 02 60 60/☎ 01 44 68 44 68 Ⓜ Bercy

Parc des Princes (2, G2) The home ground of Paris-Saint Germain (PSG), one of the best football (soccer) teams in the French first division. If playing at home, the games are usually on a Saturday night. Rugby matches are occasionally played here.

✉ 24 rue du Commandant-Guilbaud, 16e ☎ 01 42 88 02 76 for a recording; reservations ☎ 01 49 87 29 29 Ⓜ Port de St-Cloud ⊘ box office Mon-Fri 9am-8pm, Sat 10am-5pm

Stade de France

Now hallowed ground, following France's 3-0 (un, deux, trois: zéro!) victory over Brazil in the 1998 World Cup, the Stade de France at Saint Denis is a high-tech football stadium hosting both international soccer and rugby matches. ✉ rue Francis de Pressensé, Saint Denis (1, B7) ☎ 01 55 93 00 00 Ⓡ RER St-Denis

Palais Omnisports de Paris-Bercy

places to stay

There's a huge variety of accommodation in Paris, ranging from sumptuous palaces and converted 17th-century townhouses to poky little holes where you wouldn't tether your dog. And while there's something like 1500 hotels in the city, nearly 20 million visitors a year gobble up the available rooms pretty quickly. The most interesting hotels can be booked out weeks, if not months, in advance: high season is May-October, and in January and March many upmarket hotels can be busy for the fashion shows; at other times, Paris' burgeoning trade fair business can also make accommodation tight in an otherwise normal week. On the other hand, in July and particularly August, when businesses close for the summer, many hotels drop their rates to attract tourists. The best advice: book as far ahead as you can.

Room Rates

The price ranges in this chapter indicate the cost per night of a standard double room.

Deluxe	900-4000FF
Top End	500-900FF
Mid-Range	350-500FF
Budget	100-350FF

Rob Flynn

Bookings

If you get stuck, the Paris tourist office (☎ 01 49 52 53 54; 9am-8pm) at 127 ave des Champs Élysées, 8e (3, B3; Ⓜ George V), and its 3 annexes (in the Gare du Nord, Gare de Lyon and, in summer, at the base of the Tour Eiffel) can find you a place to stay for the night for a small fee. The AJF (Accueil des Jeunes en France; ☎ 01 42 77 87 80), at 119 rue St-Martin, 4e (5, B7; Ⓜ Rambuteau), can *always* find you a room, no matter what age you are; early birds get the best options. Open Monday to Friday 10am-6.45pm (Saturday to 5.45pm); long queues in summer.

Often (but not always) room rates will include breakfast – usually croissants and rolls plus tea and coffee. Make it clear on arrival whether or not you want breakfast at the hotel; most people opt for breakfast on a cafe terrace rather than in a dingy dining room.

Hotels expect you to check in by 6pm: ring if you are going to arrive any later to assure your reservation is retained. Check-out is noon.

DELUXE

L'Hôtel
Tucked away in a quiet quay-side street, L'Hôtel is the stuff of romantic Paris legends. Rock and film star patrons alike fight to sleep in the room where Oscar Wilde died a century ago or in the mirrored Art Deco room of legendary stripper Mistinguett.
✉ 13 rue des Beaux Arts, 6e (3, F9) ☎ 01 43 25 27 22; fax 01 43 25 64 81 @ reservations@l-hotel.com; www.l-hotel.com
Ⓜ St-Germain des Prés
✕ restaurant

Hôtel Costes
Jean-Louis Costes' eponymous 4-star hotel, opened in 1995, offers a 'luxurious and immoderate home away from home' to the visiting style mafia. Outfitted by Jacques Garcia in camp Second Empire castoffs, it's the current darling of the richly famous.
✉ 239 rue St-Honoré, 1er (3, C8) ☎ 01 42 44 50 00; fax 01 45 44 50 01 Ⓜ Concorde
✕ restaurant

Hôtel de Crillon
With a commanding view of the Place de la Concorde, the colonnaded Crillon (built for Louis XV in 1758) is the epitome of French luxury. The sparkling public areas are sumptuously decorated with chandeliers, original sculptures, gilt mouldings, tapestries and inlaid furniture. Ex-presidents and film stars exchange nods in the fitness centre.
✉ 10 Place de la Concorde, 8e (3, C7)
☎ 01 44 71 15 00; fax 01 44 71 15 02
@ crillon@crillon-paris.com; www.crillon-paris.com Ⓜ Concorde
✕ Les Ambassadeurs restaurant, Jardins d'Hiver tearoom

Hôtel de Lutèce
This exquisite little hotel, more country than city, is in the heart of one of Paris'

most charming quarters. The comfortable rooms are tastefully decorated, the staff are friendly and the location is probably the most desirable in all France.
✉ 65 rue St-Louis en l'Île, 4e (5, E6) ☎ 01 43 26 23 52; fax 01 43 29 60 25 Ⓜ Pont Marie

Hôtel Raphaël
Discretion is the watchword of this richly (and authentically) furnished *petit palace* (with 90 rooms, including 38 apartments), just a quick limo ride from the Champs Élysées. The view from the 7th-floor terrace restaurant is one of the best in Paris. And the mock-Gothic bar offers welcome sanctuary from the paparazzi.
✉ 17 ave Kléber, 16e (3, B2) ☎ 01 44 28 00 28; fax 01 45 01 21 50 @ www.raphael-hotel.com Ⓜ Kléber
✕ La Salle à Manger restaurant, summer terrace.

Rob Flynn

The truly palatial Hôtel de Crillon

TOP END

Hôtel Brighton

The recently renovated Brighton has wonderful views over the Jardin des Tuileries (and, from the 4th and 5th floors, over the trees to the Seine), and is handy to just about everything.

✉ 218 rue de Rivoli, 1er (3, D8) ☎ 01 47 03 61 61; fax 01 42 60 41 78 Ⓜ Tuileries

Hôtel d'Angleterre

A beautiful and very popular hotel in a quiet street close to busy blvd St-Germain and the Musée d'Orsay. The loyal clientele breakfast or brunch in the courtyard garden of this former British Embassy where Hemingway once lodged (room 14).

✉ 44 rue Jacob, 6e (3, F9) ☎ 01 42 60 34 72; fax 01 42 60 16 93 Ⓜ St-Germain des Prés

Hôtel des Deux Îles

Under the same friendly and helpful management as the Hôtel de Lutèce, the Deux Îles has tiny-but-cheerful, comfortable rooms and a great location on romantic Île St-Louis.

✉ 59 rue St-Louis en l'Île, 4e (5, E6) ☎ 01 43

Hôtel Familia

26 13 35; fax 01 43 29 60 25 Ⓜ Pont Marie

Hôtel des Grandes Écoles

Just a *boule* toss from the Place de la Contrescarpe, this popular hotel has one of the loveliest positions in the Quartier Latin. Tucked away in a courtyard off a medieval street, its courtyard garden is the perfect place to sip Pouilly Fumé on a summer evening.

✉ 65 rue du Cardinal Lemoine, 5e (5, E4) ☎ 01 43 26 79 23; fax 01 43 25 28 15 Ⓜ Cardinal Lemoine

Hôtel des Marronniers

Small, charming and spotless rooms – many with a view of St-Germain des Prés or overlooking the private garden – in the heart of the antique dealers' quarter. Scrumptious breakfasts are served in your room or under the chestnuts (*marroniers*).

✉ 21 rue Jacob, 6e (3, F9) ☎ 01 43 25 30 60; fax 01 40 46 83 56 Ⓜ St-Germain des Prés

Hôtel Familia

Choose either photogenic street views (including a glimpse of Notre Dame from some top-floor rooms) or a quiet room at the back of this charming Latin Quarter hotel. Some of the 30 rooms may be small but all are well tended by genial owners Eric and Sophie.

✉ 11 rue des Écoles, 5e (5, E4) ☎ 01 43 54 55 27; fax 01 43 29 61 77 Ⓜ Cardinal Lemoine

Hôtel Lenox St-Germain

Simple, uncluttered and comfortable rooms upstairs and a late-opening 30s-style bar downstairs attract a chic clientele.

✉ 9 rue de l'Université, 7e (3, F8) ☎ 01 42 96 10 95; fax 01 42 61 52 83 Ⓜ Rue du Bac

Hôtel Saint Christophe

This comfortable little hotel is handy to the nightlife around Place de la Contrescarpe and just a short walk from Notre Dame. The rooms away from busy rue Monge are the quietest.

✉ 17 rue Lacépède, 5e (3, J12) ☎ 01 43 31 81 54; fax 01 43 31 12 54 Ⓜ Place Monge

Hôtel des Grandes Écoles

MID-RANGE

Grand Hôtel Jeanne d'Arc

This small hotel near lovely Place du Marché Ste-Catherine is a great little pied-à-terre for your peregrinations among the museums, bars and restaurants of the Marais, Village St-Paul and Bastille.

✉ 3 rue de Jarente, 4e (5, E8) ☎ 01 48 87 62 11; fax 01 48 87 37 31 Ⓜ St-Paul

Hôtel Chopin

This 2-star hotel was built as part of one of Paris' most delightful 19th-century covered shopping arcades. It may be a little faded around the edges, but it's still enormously evocative of the *belle époque* and the welcome is always warm. Top floors are most comfortable.

✉ 46 Passage Jouffroy (entry 10 blvd Montmartre), 9e (3, B10) ☎ 01 47 70 58 10; fax 01 42 47 00 70 Ⓜ Rue Montmartre

Hôtel de L'Espérance

Just a couple of minutes walk south of lively rue Mouffetard, this quiet, pleasant and immaculately kept hotel is excellent value in a great location.

✉ 15 rue Pascal, 5e (3, K12) ☎ 01 47 07 10 99; fax 01 43 37 56 19 Ⓜ Censier Daubenton

Hôtel de Nice

Warm, family-run place right in the thick of things. The English-speaking owners make you feel right at home; guests have even been known to sunbathe on the balconies.

The Hôtel Jeanne d'Arc in the Marais

Rob Flynn

✉ 42bis rue de Rivoli, 4e (5, D7) ☎ 01 42 78 55 29; fax 01 42 78 36 07 Ⓜ Hôtel de Ville

Hôtel des Arts

Cheap and funky hotel with loads of personality (and resident parrot) in a little alley near the Grands Boulevards.

✉ 7 cité Bergère (off rue Bergère), 9e (3, B11) ☎ 01 42 46 73 30; fax 01 48 00 94 42 Ⓜ Rue Montmartre

Hôtel du Septième Art

Somewhat reminiscent of a Shinjuku love hotel, this is a fun place for movie buffs – reeking of Hollywood nostalgia and with a black-and-white movie theme throughout, right down to the tiled floors and bathrooms. A cosy place to hang your wig for a few days.

✉ 20 rue St-Paul, 4e (5, E7) ☎ 01 44 54 85 00; fax 01 42 77 69 10 Ⓜ St-Paul

Airport Hotels

If you're worried about missing your flight, rest easy by staying at one of the following airport hotels:

Roissy Charles de Gaulle

Cocoon (☎ 01 48 62 06 16; fax 01 48 62 56 97) sleep 'cabins' at CDG Terminal 1; 16hrs max
Hilton (☎ 01 49 19 77 77; fax 01 49 19 77 78)
Ibis (☎ 01 49 19 19 19; fax 01 49 19 19 21)
Novotel (☎ 01 49 19 27 27; fax 01 49 19 27 99)

Orly

Hilton (☎ 01 45 12 45 12; fax 01 45 12 45 00)
Ibis (☎ 01 46 87 33 50; fax 01 46 87 29 92)
Mercure (☎ 01 46 87 23 37; fax 01 46 87 71 92)

Hôtel Esmeralda, for a close encounter with Notre Dame

Hôtel Esmeralda

This atmospheric 15-room hotel, tucked away in a quiet street within swooning distance of Notre Dame, has been everyone's secret 'find' for years, with its picture-postcard views of Quasimodo's home, its resident cats and artist-owner Mdme Buren. Book early and book often.

✉ **4 rue St-Julien-le-Pauvre, 5e (5, C4)** ☎ 01 43 54 19 20; fax 01 40 51 00 68 Ⓜ St-Michel

Hôtel Marignan

The excellent value and free use of a fridge, microwave, washing machine and clothes dryer draws a constant stream of long-haulers to this friendly place in the heart of the Quartier Latin.

✉ **13 rue du Sommerard, 5e (5, D4)** ☎ 01 43 25 31 03 Ⓜ Maubert Mutualité

Hôtel Michelet-Odéon

Only a minute's walk from the Jardin du Luxembourg, this 42-room hotel has tasteful, generously proportioned rooms, modern bathrooms and lots of satisfied customers. Upper floors have good views over the busy Place de l'Odéon.

✉ **6 Place de l'Odéon, 6e (5, B3)** ☎ 01 46 34 27 80; fax 01 46 34 78 50 Ⓜ Odéon

Hôtel Saint Jacques

Audrey Hepburn and Cary Grant, who filmed scenes of *Charade* here, would commend the mod-cons which now complement the original 19th-century detailing (ornamented ceilings, iron staircase) of this adorable little hotel. The evening balcony views of the Panthéon are magic.

✉ **35 rue des Écoles, 5e (5, D4)** ☎ 01 43 26 82 53; fax 01 43 25 65 50 Ⓜ Maubert Mutualité

Timhôtel Montmartre (4, C5)

It may be a modern chain hotel, but the location is right: on the pretty square where Picasso and his mates changed the course of modern art in the Bateau Lavoir. Some of the rooms on the 4th and 5th floors have stunning views of the city.

✉ **11 Place Émile Goudeau, 18e** ☎ 01 42 55 74 79; fax 01 42 55 71 01 Ⓜ Abbesses

Hôtel Saint Jacques

BUDGET

Aloha Hostel

Laid-back and quiet hostel between Gare Montparnasse and the Tour Eiffel. Rooms (some with showers) have 2-6 beds. No access to rooms from 11am-5pm but reception is always open; curfew is 2am. Kitchen facilities and safe-deposit boxes are available. Good spot for singles on a budget.

✉ **1 rue Borromée, 15e (3, K5)** ☎ **01 42 73 03 03; fax 01 42 73 14 14** ✉ **www.aloha.fr** Ⓜ **Volontaires**

Auberge Internationale des Jeunes

This clean and very friendly hostel, 700m east of Place de la Bastille, attracts a young, international crowd and is very full in summer. Open 24hrs, but rooms are closed for cleaning 10am-3pm. You can book in advance, and they'll hold a bed for you if you call from the train station.

✉ **10 rue Trousseau, 11e (2, F12)** ☎ **01 47**

Hôtel Gay Lussac

00 62 00; fax 01 47 00 33 16 ✉ **aij@aijparis. com; www.aijparis.com** Ⓜ **Ledru Rollin**

Hôtel Castex

Barely a minute's stroll from Bastille, this immaculate and welcoming hotel has 27 unpretentious but comfortable (even spacious!) rooms (no TV). It's excellent value – but be prepared for some serious stair-climbing. The loyal clientele know to book well in advance.

✉ **5 rue Castex, 4e (3, G14)** ☎ **01 42 72 31 52; fax 01 42 72 57 91** Ⓜ **Bastille**

Hôtel de Nevers

Good-value and friendly budget accommodation just a short stroll from the Marais and Oberkampf neighbourhoods.

✉ **53 rue de Malte, 11e (3, D15)** ☎ **01 47 00 56 18; fax 01 43 57 77 39** Ⓜ **République**

Hôtel des Académies

This 21-room hotel located in the former artists' quarter of Montparnasse has been run by the same friendly family since 1920. It retains an authentic 1950s feel, and offers

Serviced Apartments

Staying in a serviced apartment is like staying in a hotel without all the extras, and can be cheaper for families/groups or longer stays (7 days or more).

Citadines Apparthôtels (☎ 01 41 05 79 79; fax 01 47 59 04 70; www.citadines.com) has 10 properties throughout Paris with studios and apartments catering for 1-6 people.

Hôtel et Résidence Trousseau (☎ 01 48 05 55 55; fax 01 48 05 83 97; www.hroy.com/vf/ hr/rtrousseau.htm; metro Ledru Rollin), 13 rue Trousseau, 11e (2, F12), is perfect for families or groups of friends. The kitchenette-equipped rooms or apartments for 2-6 people are large and modern.

Pensions

Pensions are the European equivalent of B&Bs, and can be an interesting alternative to hotels. Expect to pay around 200/400FF for a single/double.

Pension Au Palais Gourmand (☎ 01 45 48 24 15; fax 01 42 22 33 41; Ⓜ Vavin or Notre-Dame-des-Champs) 120 blvd Raspail, 6e (3, J8)

Pension Bairi (☎ 01 47 70 78 72; Ⓜ Poissonière) 62 rue du Faubourg Poissonière, 10e (3, B11)

Pension Ladagnous (☎ 01 43 26 79 32; Ⓜ Vavin or Notre-Dame-des-Champs) 78 rue d'Assas, 6e (5, B1)

Pension Les Marroniers (☎ 01 43 26 37 71; fax 01 43 26 07 72; Ⓜ Vavin or Notre-Dame-des-Champs) 78 rue d'Assas, 6e (5, B1)

Residence Cardinal (☎ 01 48 74 16 16; Ⓜ Liège or Place de Clichy) 4 rue Cardinal Mercier, 9e (4, E1)

clean, cheap and basic lodgings.
✉ **15 rue de la Grande Chaumière, 6e (3, K8)**
☎ **01 43 26 66 44; fax 01 43 26 03 72**
Ⓜ **Vavin**

Hôtel Gay Lussac

This family-run, 1-star place with a bit of character (and a lift) has small rooms at tiny prices; larger rooms (with shower) won't cost you much more. It's a few minutes walk from the Jardin du Luxembourg and Quartier Latin.
✉ **29 rue Gay Lussac, 5e (5, D2)** ☎ **01 43 54 23 96; fax 01 40 51 79 49** 🚉 **RER Luxembourg**

MIJE Hostels

If you're between 18-30, one of the best deals in Paris has to be the 3 popular hostels run by the Maisons Internationales des Jeunes Étudiants, all in converted 17th-century buildings in the Marais. Great digs, great locations and great prices.
✉ **11 rue du Fauconnier, 4e (5, E7)**
☎ **01 42 74 23 45; fax 01 40 27 81 64**
Ⓔ **www.mije.com**
Ⓜ **St-Paul**

Le Village Hostel

(4, D7) This fine new 26-room hostel with beamed ceilings and views of Sacré Cœur has beds in rooms for 2-6 people. All rooms have showers and WC; prices include breakfast, and kitchen facilities are available. There's also a bar and a lovely terrace for sitting outside.
✉ **20 rue d'Orsel, 18e**
☎ **01 42 64 22 02; fax 01 42 64 22 04**
Ⓜ **Anvers**

Young & Happy Hostel

This clean, very friendly, English-speaking hostel is in the happening centre of the Quartier Latin and is very popular with American and Japanese backpackers. The rooms are closed from 11am-5pm but reception is always open, and the 2am curfew is strictly enforced. The TV in the lounge area receives CNN and MTV.
✉ **80 rue Mouffetard, 5e (3, K12)** ☎ **01 45 35 09 53; fax 01 47 07 22 24** Ⓔ **smile@youngandhappy.fr; www.youngandhappy.fr**
Ⓜ **Place Monge**

Young & Happy Hostel

Rob Flynn

facts for the visitor

PRE-DEPARTURE

Travel Requirements

Passport
Visitors must carry their passport or European Union (EU) national ID card at all times.

Visa
Visas are not required by citizens of the EU, USA, Canada, New Zealand, Israel and Australia (for visits up to 3 months).

Immunisations
Immunisations are required only if you've visited an infected country in the preceding 14 days (aircraft refuelling stops not included).

Travel Insurance
A policy that covers theft, loss, flight cancellations and medical problems is a must; check with your travel agent.

Driving Licence & Permit
Visitors can drive using their home-country driving licence plus International Driving Permit (IDP).

Keeping Copies
Keep photocopies of important documents with you, separate from the originals, and leave a copy at home. You can also store details of documents in Lonely Planet's free online Travel Vault, password-protected and accessible worldwide. See the Web site at www.ekno.lonelyplanet.com.

Tourist Information Abroad

French government tourist offices (usually called Maisons de la France) can provide every imaginable sort of tourist information on Paris, as well as the rest of the country, most of it in the form of brochures. The Web address is at www.france-tourism.com and offices include the following:

Australia
(☎ 02-9231 5244; fax 02-9221 8682; frencht@ozemail.com.au) 25 Bligh St, Sydney, NSW 2000

Canada
(☎ 514-288 4264; fax 514-845 4868; mfrance@passeport.com) 1981 McGill College Ave, Suite 490, Montreal, Que H3A 2W9

South Africa
(☎ 011-880 8062; fax 011-880 7722; mdfsa@frenchdoor.co.za) Oxford Manor, 1st floor, 196 Oxford Rd, Illovo 2196

UK
(☎ 0891-244 123; fax 020-7493 6594; piccadillymdlf@demon.co.uk) 178 Piccadilly, London W1V 0AL

USA
(☎ 410-286-8310; fax 212-838 7855; info@francetourism.com) 444 Madison Ave, 16th floor, New York, NY 10022-6903

Climate & When to Go

Just go! Paris is worth visiting at any time of the year – though the weather is often unpredictable. Paris' average yearly temperature is 3-12°C (37-53°F) in January, 19°C (66°F) in July – but the mercury sometimes drops below zero in winter and can climb to 35°C (95°F) or higher in the middle of summer. April-May and September are probably the best months to see the city.

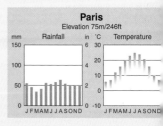

Paris
Elevation 75m/246ft

ARRIVAL & DEPARTURE

Paris can be reached by direct flights from major cities (and some minor ones) all over the globe. It's within an hour's flying time or so of major European cities such as London, Barcelona, Amsterdam, Berlin, Vienna, Prague and Rome.

Paris is also at the centre of an intricate network of road and high-speed train routes (just 3 hours to London via the Chunnel!). Wherever you're going, you can get there from Paris.

Air

Roissy Charles de Gaulle

Paris' main international airport is 30km north-east of the city centre. There are several terminals, so make sure you know which one your flight leaves from; and leave plenty of time to get your flight, as the airport is large and complex. A free *vedette* (shuttle bus) links the terminals with each other and with the Roissy train station every 5mins.

There are no left-luggage facilities at the airport. For general inquiries/flight information phone ☎ 01 48 62 22 80, 24hrs; English spoken.

Airport Access
Train Roissyrail links the city with the airport every 15mins 5.30am-midnight (45FF).

Bus Roissybus (☎ 01 48 04 18 24) links the airport with rue Scribe, Place de l'Opéra, every 15mins 5.45am-11pm (45FF).

Shuttle Air France shuttle (☎ 01 41 56 89 00) links the airport with Place Charles de Gaulle and Porte Maillot every 20mins 5.50am-11pm (60/30FF); Gare de Montparnasse and Gare de Lyon every 30mins 7am-9pm (70/35FF).

Parishuttle (☎ 0800 63 34 40) and Paris Airports Service (☎ 01 49 62 78 78; 150FF single, 85FF 2 or more people) provide door-to-door service. Pre-booking required.

Taxi The tariff to central Paris is 200-270FF, taking 30-60mins.

Orly

Orly, 18km south of the city centre, has 2 terminals – Ouest (domestic flights) and Sud (some international flights).

There are no left-luggage facilities at the airport. For general inquiries/flight information phone ☎ 01 49 75 15 15, 6am-11pm; English spoken.

Airport Access
Train The Orlyval shuttle train links Orly with RER line B at Antony, every 6mins 6am-8.30pm, Sun 7am-11pm (57/28FF).

Bus Orlybus (☎ 01 40 02 32 94) links the airport with Place Denfert Rochereau every 12mins 6am-11pm (30FF).

Jetbus (☎ 01 69 01 00 09) links Orly with the Villejuif-Louis Aragon metro stop every 15mins 6am-10pm (23FF).

Shuttle Air France shuttle (☎ 01 41 56 89 00) links the airport with Gare Montparnasse and Aérogare des Invalides every 12mins 6am-11pm (45/23FF).

Parishuttle (☎ 0800 63 34 40) and Paris Airports Service (☎ 01 49 62 78 78; 115FF single, 75FF 2 or more people) provide door-to-door service. Pre-booking required.

Taxi The tariff to central Paris is 120-175FF, taking 20-30mins.

Train

Paris has 6 major train stations: Gare d'Austerlitz, Gare de l'Est, Gare de Lyon, Gare du Nord, Gare Montparnasse and Gare St Lazare. Train information is available for mainline services on ☎ 08 36 35 35 35 and for suburban and RER services on ☎ 01 53 90 20 20 or ☎ 01 53 90 10 10 (recording); you can also find service info and ticket prices at www.sncf.fr online.

Eurostar

(☎ 08 36 35 35 39; UK ☎ 0990 186 186) The passenger train service through the Channel Tunnel arrives and departs from Paris Gare du Nord bound for London's Waterloo Station. The trip takes 3hrs station to station; with the time zone change between France and England, the elapsed time is 2hrs Paris-London and 4hrs London-Paris. The confusing fare structure ranges from UK£79-169 return from London, depending on when you travel (have a look at the Web site at www.eurostar.com).

Customs

No guns, ammunition, illegal drugs or nuclear waste.

Duty Free

You can no longer buy goods at duty-free prices if travelling only between the member countries of the EU.

The usual allowances apply: tobacco (200 cigarettes, 50 cigars or 250g of loose tobacco), alcohol (1L of strong liquor or 2L of less than 22% alcohol by volume; 2L of wine), coffee (500g or 200g of extracts) and perfume (50g of perfume and 250mL of toilet water).

Departure Tax

Departure tax is prepaid – it is included in the price of your ticket.

GETTING AROUND

Paris has a fast, efficient and safe public transport system, though strikes may affect services from time to time. Wherever you go in Paris, you're never further than 500m from a metro station, and probably even closer to a bus route. Most of the system is operated by the RATP (Régie Autonome des Transports Parisians). In summer the Batobus river taxi plies the Seine between the Tour Eiffel and Notre Dame.

Travel Passes

The Mobilis and Paris Visite passes allow unlimited travel on the metro, RER and SNCF suburban lines, buses, the Noctambus system, trams and the Montmartre funicular railway. Mobilis allows unlimited travel for 1 day in 2 (Paris) or 8 (Île de France) zones. Paris Visite passes are valid for 1-5 consecutive days of travel in either 3, 5 or 8-zone versions. Both passes are available at larger metro and RER stations, at SNCF bureaux in Paris and at the airports.

Train

Paris' underground network is simple to use and is generally the fastest way of getting around the city. It consists of 2 separate but linked systems: the Métropolitain, known as the *métro*, which has 14 lines and over 300 stations; and the RER, a network of 5 suburban services that pass through the city centre. Normally, you'd only use the RER if you wanted to cover large distances quickly, eg St-Michel to Tour Eiffel. Free metro/RER maps are available at metro ticket windows.

The metro runs from around 5.30am-midnight; trains run every 5mins or so. Each line is designated by a number, a colour and a *direction*, or final destination, which ensures you're on the right platform.

For information on the metro, RER and bus system, call the RATP's 24hr inquiries number ☎ 08 36 68 77 14 (French) or ☎ 08 36 68 41 14 (English); online, check www.ratp.fr for details.

Information on SNCF's suburban services (including certain RER lines) is available on ☎ 01 53 90 20 20 or ☎ 01 53 90 10 10 (recording); online, check the www.sncf.fr Web site for details.

Tickets

Tickets for travel within the Paris city limits on the metro and RER network cost 8FF if bought individually (*billet*) and 55FF for a *carnet* of 10. Children under 4 travel free; children under 10 half-fare. Tickets are sold at windows and machines at every metro station, though not always at each and every entrance.

Carry your ticket with you until you have exited the station, as spot checks (and spot fines) are frequent.

Bus

Bus may be a little slower on long trips across the city, but it can be a much better way of seeing the sights while you're travelling. Regular services run frequently from around 7am-8.30pm, but are reduced at night and on Sundays. As your bus approaches, signal the driver to stop by waving. Any journey that starts and ends within Paris costs 1 metro ticket – cancel it in the machine provided onboard. If you have a Mobilis or Paris Visite pass, just flash it at the driver.

Noctambus

The Noctambus (☎ 08 36 68 77 14) network operates after the metro has shut down for the night. Buses on the service's 18 lines depart every hour on the half-hour 1.30-5.30am from just west of the Hôtel de Ville and cover most of the city. Look for the symbol of a little black owl silhouetted against a yellow moon. Tickets costs 30FF, or use your Mobilis or Paris Visite pass.

Taxi

Parisian taxi drivers have a reputation for arrogance but, within reason, it's all part of the fun. Radio-dispatched taxi companies, on call 24hrs, include: Taxis Bleus (English-speaking operators ☎ 01 49 36 10 10), G7 Radio (☎ 01 47 39 47 39; English ☎ 01 41 27 66 99; airport travel ☎ 01 41 27 66 66), Alpha Taxis (☎ 01 45 85 85 85), Artaxi (☎ 01 42 08 64 59) and Taxis-Radio 7000 (☎ 01 42 70 00 42).

Fares & Charges

The *prise en charge* (flag-fall fee) is 13FF. Within the city, it costs 3.45FF/km for travel Mon-Sat, 7am-7pm. At night, on Sundays and holidays it's 5.70FF/km. It costs 135FF/hr to have a taxi wait for you.

There's an extra 10FF charge for taking a fourth passenger – but always ask permission first, as many drivers are reluctant to take more than 3 people (for insurance reasons). Each piece of baggage over 5kg costs 6FF and from certain train stations there's a 5FF supplement. The usual tip is just a few francs no matter what the fare. Make reservations for peak-hour and airport travel.

Approximate Fares

Notre Dame to Jardin du Luxembourg	15FF
Notre Dame to Musée d'Orsay	20FF
Châtelet to Bastille	20FF
Gare du Nord to Châtelet	25FF
Hôtel de Ville to Arc de Triomphe	30FF
Sacré Cœur to Tour Eiffel	30FF
Bastille to Tour Eiffel	50FF

Car & Motorcycle

Driving in Paris is difficult but not impossible by any means – except for the nervy, faint-hearted or indecisive. The fastest way to get across Paris is often the *périphérique* (the ring road or beltway that encircles the city) or the *quais* (the left bank goes west; the right, east).

In most parts of Paris you have to pay 10FF/hr to park your car on the street – look for white-outlined spaces marked *payant*; yellow markings mean no parking. Large municipal parking garages charge around 12-15FF/hr or, for periods of 12 to 24hrs, 80-130FF. Parking fines are usually 75 or 200FF.

Road Rules

Vehicles drive on the right-hand side of the road; seat belts are compulsory (front and back); and motorcyclists must wear helmets. The minimum driving age is 18.

Vehicles on your right always have priority, even on major roads and in roundabouts.

Speed Limits 50km/h in built-up areas, 90km/h on undivided highways, 110km/h on dual carriageways and 130km/h on autoroutes.

Drink-Driving The blood-alcohol limit of 0.05% is enforced with random breath checks and severe punishments.

Car Rental

The major companies – Avis (☎ 08 02 05 05 05), Europcar (☎ 08 03 35 23 52) and Hertz (☎ 01 39 38 38 38) – have reservations centres and offices in the city and Roissy airport. ADA (☎ 08 36 68 40 02) and Rent A Car 7 (☎ 08 36 69 46 95) are smaller companies. The minimum age to rent a car is 25. Book well ahead if you want to hire a car with automatic transmission, as most rental cars are manual.

Motoring Organisations

The Automobile Club de l'Île de France (☎ 01 40 55 43 00; acif@autoclubs-associes.tm.fr), 14 Ave de la Grande Armée, 17e (3, A2), sells insurance coverage and can provide basic maps and itinerary suggestions.

PRACTICAL INFORMATION
Tourist Information

The main tourist office (☎ 01 49 52 53 54 or, for information in English, ☎ 01 44 29 12 12) is at 127 ave des Champs Élysées, 8e (3, B3),

open 9am-8pm (Sunday in winter 11am-6pm). There are tourist office annexes in the Gare du Nord (2, C10; ☎ 01 45 26 94 82) and the Gare de Lyon (2, G12; ☎ 01 43 43 33 24) open daily, except Sunday and holidays, 8am-8pm. The annexe at the base of the Tour Eiffel (3, F2; ☎ 01 45 51 22 15) is open from 2 May to September daily (including holidays) 11am-6pm.

The Île de France tourist office (☎ 01 42 44 10 50) is in the lower level of the Carrousel du Louvre shopping mall (3, E9) next to IM Pei's inverted glass pyramid. It is open daily, except Tuesday, 10am-7pm.

Embassies

Australia
(☎ 01 40 59 33 00) 4 rue Jean Rey, 15e (3, F2; Ⓜ Bir Hakeim)
Canada
(☎ 01 44 43 29 00) 35 ave Montaigne, 8e (3, C4; Ⓜ Alma Marceau)
New Zealand
(☎ 01 45 00 24 11) rue Léonard de Vinci, 16e (3, B1; Ⓜ Victor Hugo)
South Africa
(☎ 01 53 59 23 23) 59 Quai d'Orsay, 7e (3, E6; Ⓜ Invalides)
UK
(☎ 01 44 51 31 00, 24hrs in an emergency ☎ 01 42 66 29 79) 16 rue d'Anjou, 8e (3, C7; Ⓜ Concorde)
USA
(☎ 01 43 12 23 47, 24hrs in an emergency ☎ 01 43 12 49 48) 2 rue St-Florentin, 1er (3, C7; Ⓜ Concorde)

Money

Currency
The unit of currency is the French franc (FF), which is divided into 100 centimes. Coins come in 1, 2, 5, 10 and 20FF, and 5, 10, 20 and 50 centimes. Notes come in 20, 50, 100, 200 and 500FF denominations.

Prices are generally marked in both francs and euro (ë), the new currency of the EU, although euro notes and coins won't begin circulating until January 2002. One euro is worth 6.56FF.

Travellers Cheques
Except at exchange bureaux and the Banque de France, expect to pay a minimum charge of 20-30FF to cash travellers cheques. American Express (3, B8; ☎ 01 47 77 70 00), 14 rue Scribe, 9e, does not charge a commission on its own travellers cheques. American Express (in US dollars or French francs) and Visa travellers cheques can also be cashed at many post offices.

Eurocheques
Eurocheques are guaranteed up to a certain limit. When cashing them (eg at post offices), you will be asked to show your Eurocheque card, and passport or ID card. Eurocheques may be refused because of the relatively large commissions.

Credit Cards
Visa (often called *Carte Bleu* in France) is the most widely accepted credit card, followed by MasterCard. American Express and Diners Club cards are only accepted at upmarket establishments. For lost cards contact:

American Express	☎ 01 47 77 70 00
Diners Club	☎ 01 49 06 17 50
MasterCard	☎ 0800 90 13 87
Visa	☎ 0800 90 11 79

Changing Money
Foreign cash is not the best way to carry money in France; it's far better to bring francs with you. Banks and exchange bureaux often give poorer rates for cash than travellers cheques.

Major train stations and hotels have exchange facilities which operate evenings, weekends and holidays. Banque de France, France's central bank, offers the best exchange rates, but it does not accept Eurocheques or provide credit card cash advances. Many post offices perform exchange transactions for a middling rate.

ATMs

There seems to be at least 2 or 3 banks on every major corner, all willing to give you francs at very good exchange rates – as long as your card is linked to the Cirrus and/or Maestro networks; do this before you leave home – and make sure you know your PIN number. Some ATMs may accept PINs with 4 digits only; if you have a problem, try another bank. You should also check your daily withdrawal limit before you leave home.

Tipping

French law requires that restaurant, cafe and hotel bills include a mandatory service charge of 10-15%, so a *pourboire* (tip) is neither necessary nor expected in most cases. However, most people leave a few francs in restaurants, unless the service was bad. They rarely tip in cafes and bars when they've just had a coffee or a drink.

Discounts & Discount Cards

Concessions (usually 30-50%) abound for youth, students and seniors on everything from transport to museums. Bring whatever concession ID you have from home and flash it every time you pull out your wallet.

Student & Youth Cards

The International Student Identity Card (ISIC) is widely accepted throughout France and affords half-price admissions, discounted air and ferry tickets, and cheap meals in student cafeterias. Many places stipulate a maximum age, usually 24 or 25.

Seniors' Cards

Reduced-entry prices are charged for people over 60 at most cultural centres, including museums, galleries and public theatres. SNCF issues the Carte Senior to those over 60, with reductions of 20-50% on train tickets.

Opening Hours

Opening hours for shops, banks, museums and restaurants can seem unpredictable in Paris. Many places are closed on Sunday and either Monday or Tuesday, and many also close for lunch (usually 12.30-2.30pm). Many restaurants close before 11pm; on the other hand, many museums have *nocturnes* or late opening hours at least one night per week.

Banks

Mon-Fri 9am-4.30pm and some branches Saturday morning. Some banks close for lunch.

Post Offices

Mon-Fri 8am-7pm, Sat 8am-noon

Shops

Mon-Sat 9/10am-6.30/7pm; some open Sunday mornings Jul-Aug and to 10pm once a week.

Pharmacies

Mon-Sat 9am-6pm

Tourist Sites

Hours vary widely, but 9am-5.30pm is standard for smaller attractions; most museums close Monday or Tuesday.

Public Holidays

New Year's Day	1 Jan
Easter Sunday	Mar/Apr
Easter Monday	Mar/Apr
May Day	1 May
Victory in Europe Day	8 May

Ascension Thursday	May
Whit Sunday/Whit Monday	May/June
Bastille Day	14 July
Assumption Day	15 Aug
All Saints' Day	1 Nov
Armistice Day	11 Nov
Christmas Day	25 Dec

Time

France is 1hr ahead of GMT/UTC. During daylight-saving it is 2hrs ahead. At noon in Paris it's:

    3am in Los Angeles
    6am in New York
    11am in London
    9pm in Sydney

Electricity

Voltage is 220V AC, 50Hz. Plugs have 2 or 3 round pins; adapters are best brought from home but can be bought at FNAC in Les Halles and BHV.

Weights & Measures

France invented and still uses the metric system – though it's still possible to order by the *livre* (pound, 500g). See the conversion table on page 121.

Post

La Poste (☎ 08 01 63 02 01) runs the country's mail system.

The main post office (☎ 01 40 28 20 00) at 52 rue du Louvre, 1er (3, D11), is 5 blocks north of the eastern corner of the Louvre.

Sending Mail

Stamps are sold at post office counters, open Monday to Friday 8am-7pm, Saturday 8am-noon; the main post office is open 24hrs.

Telephone

French telephone numbers generally have 10 digits, the first 2 being the area code. Dial all 10 digits for calls within France; drop the initial zero when calling from outside France. The country code for France is ☎ 33.

Phonecards

Most public telephones require a phonecard – *télécarte* – which can be purchased at post offices, *tabacs* (tobacconists), supermarket check-out counters, SNCF ticket windows, Paris metro stations and anywhere you see a blue sticker reading '*télé-carte en vente ici*'. Cards worth 50 calling units cost 49FF; those worth 120 units are 97.50FF.

Many cafes and restaurants have privately owned and/or coin-operated Point Phones. To find a Point Phone, look for blue-on-white window stickers bearing the Point Phone emblem.

Lonely Planet's eKno Communication Card, specifically designed for travellers, provides competitive international calls (avoid using it for local calls), messaging services and free email. The toll-free eKno number to call when you are in France is ☎ 0800 91 20 66.

Mobile Phones

France uses the GSM cellular phone system, compatible with phones sold in the UK, Australia and most of Asia, but not those from North America or Japan. To use your cellular in France, your service provider will need to have a roaming agreement with a counterpart in France. Check before you leave home.

Useful Numbers

Operator/Directory Inquiries	☎ 12
Int'l Directory Inquiries	☎ 00 33 12
+ international dialling code of the country (use 11 in place of 1 for US and Canada)	
Int'l Operator	☎ 00 33
+ international dialling code of country	
Int'l Dialling Code	☎ 00

Reverse-Charge Calls

Australia	☎ 0800 99 00 61	Telstra
	☎ 0800 99 20 61	Optus
Canada	☎ 0800 99 00 16	
Ireland	☎ 0800 99 03 53	
New Zealand	☎ 0800 99 00 64	
UK	☎ 0800 99 00 44	BT
	☎ 0800 99 09 44	Mercury
USA	☎ 0800 99 00 11	AT&T
	☎ 0800 99 00 19	MCI
	☎ 0800 99 00 87	Sprint
	☎ 0800 99 00 13	Worldcom

International Codes

Australia	☎ 61
Canada	☎ 1
Japan	☎ 81
New Zealand	☎ 64
South Africa	☎ 27
UK	☎ 44
USA	☎ 1

Email/www

After resisting the 'Anglo' Internet for several years, the French have now seized *le web* with typical enthusiasm and flair. To get your email fix or browse the Web, drop into one of the many cybercafes mushrooming around town (see p. 85) or, if you're carrying your own machine, take out a subscription with a local ISP.

Internet service providers

The local dial-in number for AOL is ☎ 01 40 64 16 70 and Compuserve ☎ 01 41 02 03 04.

Club Internet
    ☎ 0 801 800 900; www.club-internet.fr
Wanadoo
    ☎ 0 801 105 105; www.wanadoo.fr

Useful Sites

Start at Lonely Planet's Web sites (www.lonelyplanet.com for information in English and www.lonely planet.fr for information in French) for an introduction to Paris, the latest travel news, tips from other travellers and links to useful travel resources. You could also try:

Good Morning Paris
    www.goodmorningparis
Metropole Paris
    www.metropoleparis.com
The Paris Pages
    www.paris.org
Paris Tourist office
    www.paris-touristoffice.com

Doing Business

Le Monde and *Le Figaro* are the foremost local publications on business and finance.

Many hotels provide business facilities, including conference rooms, secretarial services, fax and photocopying services, use of computers and private office space. Some also provide specialist translation services.

The business centre (☎ 01 48 62 22 90; fax 01 48 62 61 29) inside terminal 1 of Roissy Charles de Gaulle airport has catered meeting rooms, offices and business equipment available.

Newspapers & Magazines

Newspapers

Paris' main daily newspapers are *Le Monde*, *Liberation* and *Le Figaro*.

Magazines

Paris' most popular magazines are *L'Express*, *Le Point*, *Le Nouvel* and *Observateur*.

Sport

The daily devoted to sport is *L'Équipe*.

English-language Papers & Magazines

English-language newspapers widely available in Paris are the *International Herald Tribune*,

European, The Times, Guardian, USA Today, Financial Times, Newsweek, Time and the *Economist*.

English Entertainment Listings

There's a 'Time Out' supplement in the weekly *Pariscope* (see p. 86).

Radio

BBC World Service/BBC for Europe
(648 AM) – news & views
Voice of America
(1197 AM)
Radio France Internationale
(738 AM) – English news and music 3-4pm

TV

There are 5 free-to-air channels – 3 state-owned (France 2, F3 and Arte/La Cinquième) and 2 commercial (TF1 and M6). In addition there is a subscription movie channel, Canal+, plus a range of cable and satellite offerings, with programming from CNN and the BBC amongst others. The main news bulletin is at 8pm on TF1 and France 2, and 8.30pm on Arte. Programming on the free-to-air stations is entirely in French, though there's the odd movie or serial in English with French subtitles.

Many cable-equipped hotels offer CNN and BBC news channels. While most English-language programs are dubbed into French for the local audience, films and series are often shown in English (look for the letters 'vo' – *version originale*), with French subtitles.

Photography & Video

Print and slide film are both widely available.

Film is susceptible to heat, so protect your film by keeping it cool and having it processed as soon as possible. The best photographs are taken early in the morning or late in the afternoon, especially in summer when the sun's glare tends to wash out colours.

France uses the Phase Alternative Line (PAL) system, which isn't compatible with other standards unless converted.

Photography is rarely forbidden, except in museums and art galleries, though in some areas police may move you along if you set up a tripod.

Health

Precautions

Paris' tap water is perfectly safe to drink, although it does have quite a strong chlorine taste.

Insurance & Medical Treatment

EU residents are covered for emergency medical treatment throughout the EU. The coverage provided by most private US health insurance policies continues if you travel abroad, at least for a limited period. Canadians covered by the Régie de l'Assurance-Maladie du Québec can benefit from certain reimbursement agreements with France's national health-care system. If you're not covered by your local health-insurance scheme, travel insurance is advisable.

Medical Services

There are some 50 *assistance publique* (public health service) hospitals in Paris. If you need an ambulance, call ☎ 15 or ☎ 01 45 67 50 50. For emergency treatment, call Urgences Médicales on ☎ 01 48 28 40 04 or SOS Médecins on ☎ 01 47 07 77 77. Both offer 24hr house calls. Some possibilities are:

Hôpital Américain
(☎ 01 46 41 25 25) 63 blvd Victor Hugo, 17e (2, B4; Ⓜ Porte Maillot)

Hôpital Franco-Britannique
(☎ 01 46 39 22 22) 3 rue Barbès, 17e (2, B4; Ⓜ Anatole-France)

Hôtel Dieu
(☎ 01 42 34 82 34) Place du Parvis Notre Dame, 4e (5, C5; Ⓜ Cité)

Dental Emergencies

La Pitié-Salpêtrière, rue Bruand, 13e (2, H11), is the only dental hospital with extended hours. The after-hours entrance, open from 5.30pm-8.30am, is at 47 blvd de l'Hôpital.

SOS Dentaire (☎ 01 43 37 51 00), 87 blvd de Port Royal, 13e (2, H9), is a private dentists' office that offers its services when most dentists are off duty: Mon-Fri 8am-11.45pm, weekends and holidays 9am-12.10pm, 2.20-7.10pm and 8-11.40pm.

Pharmacies & Drugs

There's a pharmacy on nearly every corner of Paris – look for the green neon crosses. Some chemists with longer opening hours are:

Dérhy/Pharmacie des Champs
(☎ 01 45 62 02 41) 84 ave des Champs Élysées, 8e (3, B4); open 24hrs

Dérhy/Pharmacie des Halles
(☎ 01 42 72 03 23) 10 blvd de Sébastopol, 4e (5, B6); open 9am-midnight (from noon Sun and holidays)

Pharmacie Européenne de la Place de Clichy
(☎ 01 48 74 65 18) 6 Place de Clichy, 17e (4, E1); open 24hrs

HIV/AIDS

Condoms are available from chemists, convenience stores and vending machines in some toilets.

For information on free and anonymous HIV-testing centres (centres de dépistage) in and around Paris, ring the 24hr SIDA Info Service toll-free on ☎ 0800 84 08 00. FACTS-Line (☎ 01 44 93 16 69), in operation Monday, Wednesday and Friday 6-10am, is an English-language help line for those with HIV or AIDS.

Emergency Numbers

Ambulance	☎ 15
Police	☎ 17
Fire Brigade	☎ 18
Rape Crisis Hotline	☎ 0 800 059 595
Poisoning	☎ 01 40 05 48 48
Legal Advice	☎ 08 03 39 63 00

Toilets

Public toilets are signposted as toilettes or WC. Gone are the days of the vespassiennes (urinals) in the street, but Paris still has a number of fine-looking public toilets from the belle époque (at Place de la Madeleine, for example). Paris' coin-operated public toilets are cheap, clean and plentiful. Open from early morning to 10pm, you get 15mins of heated luxury for just 2FF, and the entire unit is cleaned and disinfected after each use (no need to flush). Children under 10 should be accompanied by an adult, and people with disabilities may need assistance.

Safety Concerns

In general, Paris is a safe city and occurrences of random street assaults are rare. Nonviolent crime (such as pickpocketing and thefts from handbags or packs) is a problem wherever there are crowds, especially crowds of tourists. Places in which to be especially careful include Montmartre, Pigalle, the areas around Forum des Halles and the Centre Pompidou, on the metro at rush hour and even the Quartier Latin. Be especially wary of children; kids who jostle up against you in the crowds may be diving into your bag with professional aplomb at the same instant.

Metro stations which are probably best avoided late at night include Châtelet Les Halles (with its seemingly endless corridors), Château Rouge in Montmartre, Gare du Nord, Strasbourg St-Denis, Réaumur Sébastopol and Montparnasse Bienvenüe. *Bornes d'alarme* (alarm boxes) are located in the centre of each metro/RER platform and in some station corridors.

Lost Property

All lost objects found anywhere in Paris – except those discovered on trains or in railway stations – are eventually brought to the city's infamous Bureau des Objets Trouvés (Lost Property Office; ☎ 01 55 76 20 20), 36 rue des Morillons, 15e (2, H6), run by the Préfecture de Police. The lost property office is open 8.30am-5pm on Monday, Wednesday and Friday, to 8pm Tuesday and Thursday. In July and August, daily closing time is 5pm.

Items lost in the metro are held by station agents for 1 day before being sent to the Bureau des Objets Trouvés. Anything found on trains or in railway stations is taken to the *objets trouvés* bureau – usually attached to the left-luggage office – of the relevant train station.

Women Travellers

Paris is generally a safe city, and women travelling alone rarely attract unwanted attention. Of course, you should take the normal big-city precautions at night, especially leaving bars and clubs. If you do experience unacceptable behaviour, *'Laissez-moi tranquille!'* is a firm but relatively polite way of saying 'Leave me alone!'

The women-only Maison des Femmes (☎ 01 43 43 41 13), 163 rue de Charenton, 12e (2, G12), is a meeting place for women of all ages and nationalities. It's open Wednesday, Friday and Saturday 4-7pm; cafe Friday 7-10pm.

The contraceptive pill is available on prescription only, so a visit to the doctor is necessary. Tampons are available from chemists and supermarkets.

Gay & Lesbian Travellers

France is one of Europe's most liberal countries when it comes to homosexuality, in part because of the long French tradition of public tolerance towards groups of people who choose not to live by conventional social codes. France's lesbian scene is much less public than its gay counterpart and is centred mainly around women's cafes and bars.

Information & Organisations

The best listing of gay clubs, bars and associations is in *e.m@le*, which is published weekly and free at gay venues or 8FF at newsagents. Others with fewer listings include *VIP*, *Illico* and *Idol*. Lesbian publications include *Lesbia* (monthly, 25FF) and *Les Nanas* (bimonthly, free). The Web site at www.citegay.com is useful.

Most of France's major gay organisations are based in Paris and include the following:

ActUp Paris
(☎ 01 48 06 13 89) 45 rue Sedaine, 11e (2, F12; Ⓜ Voltaire); www.actupp.org

Association des Médecins Gais
(☎ 01 48 05 81 71) Wed 6-8pm, Sat 2-4pm
Centre Gai et Lesbien (CGL)
(☎ 01 43 57 21 47) 3 rue Keller, 11e (2, F12; Ⓜ Ledru Rollin)
Écoute Gaie
(☎ 01 44 93 01 02) Hotline Mon-Fri 6-10pm, Sat 6-8pm

Senior Travellers

Senior citizens are entitled to discounts in France on things like public transport, museum admission fees etc, provided they show proof of age. In some cases a special pass is needed.

Disabled Travellers

Wheelchair Access

France is not particularly well equipped for the *handicapés* (disabled): kerb ramps are few and far between, older public facilities and bottom-end hotels often lack lifts, and the Paris metro, most of it built decades ago, is hopeless. But physically challenged people who would like to visit Paris can overcome these problems. Most hotels with 2 or more stars are equipped with lifts, and Michelin's *Guide Rouge* indicates hotels with lifts and facilities for disabled people.

In recent years the SNCF has made efforts to make its trains more accessible to people with physical disabilities. Details are available in SNCF's booklet *Guide du Voyageur à Mobilité Réduite*. You can also contact SNCF Accessibilité on ☎ 0800 15 47 53 (toll-free).

In some places vehicles outfitted for people in wheelchairs provide transport within the city. Details are available from the Groupement pour l'Insertion des Personnes Handicapées Physiques (☎ 01 41 83 15 15), 98 rue de la Porte Jaune, 92210 Saint Cloud.

Useful Publications

Access in Paris provides a good overview of facilities available to disabled travellers in Paris; published by RADAR (UK ☎ +44 020-7250 3222), 12 City Forum, 250 City Rd, London EC1V 8AF.

Tourisme pour Tout le Monde is available from the Paris tourist office (☎ 0800 03 37 48 for advice in French) for 60FF.

Language

Parisians are used to English-speaking visitors and will usually respond in kind to a polite request. Your best bet is to begin with whatever French you can muster, even if it's *Excusez-moi, madame/monsieur, parlez-vous anglais?* – 'Excuse me, madam/sir, do you speak English?'

For more useful words and phrases than we have space for here, see Lonely Planet's *French phrasebook*.

Hello/Good morning	*Bonjour.*
Good evening	*Bonsoir.*
Goodbye	*Au revoir.*
Yes	*Oui.*
No	*Non.*
Maybe	*Peut-être.*
That's good/I like it	*C'est bon!*
Please	*S'il vous plaît.*
Thank you	*Merci.*
You're welcome	*Je vous en prie.*
Excuse me	*Excusez-moi.*
I don't understand	*Je ne comprends pas.*
I'm sorry/Forgive me	*Pardon.*
Just a moment	*Un instant, s'il vous plaît.*
OK	*D'accord!*
How much is it?	*C'est combien?*

Conversion Table

Clothing Sizes

Measurements approximate only; try before you buy.

Women's Clothing

Aust/NZ	8	10	12	14	16	18
Europe	36	38	40	42	44	46
Japan	5	7	9	11	13	15
UK	8	10	12	14	16	18
USA	6	8	10	12	14	16

Women's Shoes

Aust/NZ	5	6	7	8	9	10
Europe	35	36	37	38	39	40
France only	35	36	38	39	40	42
Japan	22	23	24	25	26	27
UK	3½	4½	5½	6½	7½	8½
USA	5	6	7	8	9	10

Men's Clothing

Aust/NZ	92	96	100	104	108	112
Europe	46	48	50	52	54	56
Japan	S		M	M		L
UK	35	36	37	38	39	40
USA	35	36	37	38	39	40

Men's Shirts (Collar Sizes)

Aust/NZ	38	39	40	41	42	43
Europe	38	39	40	41	42	43
Japan	38	39	40	41	42	43
UK	15	15½	16	16½	17	17½
USA	15	15½	16	16½	17	17½

Men's Shoes

Aust/NZ	7	8	9	10	11	12
Europe	41	42	43	44½	46	47
Japan	26	27	27.5	28	29	30
UK	7	8	9	10	11	12
USA	7½	8½	9½	10½	11½	12½

Weights & Measures

Length & Distance

1 inch = 2.54cm
1cm = 0.39 inches
1m = 3.3ft
1ft = 0.3m
1km = 0.62 miles
1 mile = 1.6km

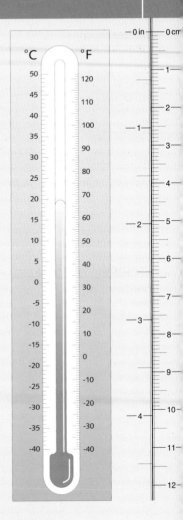

Weight

1kg = 2.2lb
1lb = 0.45kg
1g = 0.04oz
1oz = 28g

Volume

1 litre = 0.26 US gallons
1 US gallon = 3.8 litres
1 litre = 0.22 imperial gallons
1 imperial gallon = 4.55 litres

THE AUTHOR

Rob Flynn

In the twilight of the last millennium, Sydney-born Rob Flynn headed 'up-over' to the City of Light in search of fame, fortune and love. Well, one out of three ain't bad ... Now a resident of the 3e, he takes his *café noir*, knows his *cou* from his *cul*, and has *foie gras* on the shelf next to the Vegemite. This book owes much to the help of his knowledgeable *copains* and *la femme de sa vie – mille mercis*.

ABOUT LONELY PLANET GUIDEBOOKS

The story begins with a classic travel adventure: Tony and Maureen Wheeler's 1972 journey across Europe and Asia to Australia. Useful information about the overland trail did not exist at that time, so Tony and Maureen published the first Lonely Planet guidebook to meet a growing need.

From a kitchen table, then from a tiny office in Melbourne, Australia, Lonely Planet has become the largest independent travel publisher in the world, an international company with offices in Melbourne, Oakland (USA), London (UK) and Paris (France).

Today there are over 400 titles, including travel guides, city maps, cycling guides, first time travel guides, healthy travel guides, travel atlases, diving guides, pictorial books, phrasebooks, restaurant guides, travel literature, walking guides and world food guides.

At Lonely Planet we believe that travellers can make a positive contribution to the countries they visit – if they respect their host communities and spend their money wisely. Since 1986 a percentage of the income from books has been donated to aid projects and human rights campaigns.

ABOUT THE CONDENSED GUIDES

Other Lonely Planet Condensed guides include: *Amsterdam* (due July 2000), *California, Crete, London, New York City* and *Sydney*.

ABOUT THIS BOOK

Series developed by Diana Saad • Edited by Janet Austin • Design by Andrew Weatherill • Layout by Vicki Beale • Publishing Manager Mary Neighbour • Cover design by Indra Kilfoyle and Simon Bracken • Maps by Charles Rawlings-Way • Software engineering by Dan Levin • Thanks to Brett Pascoe, Emma Miller, Fiona Croyden, Gabrielle Green, Steve Fallon, Tim Uden, Trudi Canavan, Zahia Hafs and *tout le monde à* LP Paris

LONELY PLANET ONLINE

www.lonelyplanet.com or AOL keyword: lp
Lonely Planet's award-winning Web site has insider info on hundreds of destinations from Amsterdam to Zimbabwe, complete with interactive maps and colour photographs. You'll also find the latest travel news, recent reports from travellers on the road, guidebook upgrades and a lively bulletin board where you can meet fellow travellers, swap recommendations and seek advice.

PLANET TALK

Our FREE quarterly printed newsletter is full of tips from travellers and anecdotes from Lonely Planet authors. Every issue is packed with up-to-date travel news and advice, and includes a postcard from Lonely Planet co-founder Tony Wheeler, mail from travellers, a look at life on the road through the eyes of a Lonely Planet author, topical health advice, prizes for the best travel yarn, news about forthcoming Lonely Planet events and a complete list of Lonely Planet books and products.

To join our mailing list, email us at: go@lonelyplanet.co.uk (UK, Europe and Africa residents); info@lonelyplanet.com (North and South America residents); talk2us@lonelyplanet.com.au (the rest of the world); or contact any Lonely Planet office.

COMET

Our FREE monthly email newsletter brings you all the latest travel news, features, interviews, competitions, destination ideas, travellers' tips & tales, Q&As, raging debates and related links. Find out what's new on the Lonely Planet Web site and which books are about to hit the shelves.

Subscribe from your desktop: www.lonelyplanet.com/comet

LONELY PLANET OFFICES

Australia
PO Box 617, Hawthorn, Victoria 3122
☎ 03 9819 1877 fax 03 9819 6459
email: talk2us@lonelyplanet.com.au

USA
150 Linden St, Oakland, CA 94607
☎ 510 893 8555 TOLL FREE: 800 275 8555
fax 510 893 8572
email: info@lonelyplanet.com

UK
10a Spring Place, London NW5 3BH
☎ 020 7428 4800 fax 020 7428 4828
email: go@lonelyplanet.co.uk

France
1 rue du Dahomey, 75011 Paris
☎ 01 55 25 33 00 fax 01 55 25 33 01
email: bip@lonelyplanet.fr
minitel: 3615 lonelyplanet

**World Wide Web: www.lonelyplanet.com & www.lonelyplanet.fr or AOL keyword: lp
Lonely Planet Images: lpi@lonelyplanet.com.au**

index

See separate indexes for Places to Eat (p. 126), Places to Stay (p. 127), Shopping (p. 127) and Sights (p.128, includes map references).

PLACES TO EAT

PLACES TO STAY

SHOPPING

sights index